IF ONLY I WERE GOD

One Man's Solution to the Problem of Pain and Suffering

FRANK M. FANELLA

ISBN: 978-1-969422-61-4 (Paperback)
978-1-969422-62-1 (Ebook)

Editor: Bridget Chambers
Proofreader and Interior Book Layout: Amy Rice
Cover Designer: Geremy Wood
Author Photo Credit: Carlos Pablo Budassi

The views expressed in this book are solely those of the author and do not necessarily reflect the views of the publisher, and the publisher hereby disclaims any responsibility of them.

Olympus Story House
www.olympusstoryhouse.com

CONTENT

To my children, Noelle, Brenda, and Frankie,
and to all children of God.

INTRODUCTION

"Save me, O God, for the waters threaten my life;
I am sunk in the abysmal swamp where there is no foothold;
I have reached the watery depths;
The flood overwhelms me.
I am wearied with calling, my throat is parched;
My eyes have failed with looking for my God."
Book of Psalms, Psalm 69

"For what man knows God's counsel,
or who can conceive what our Lord intends?"
Wisdom, Ch 9:13

Our God is a God of love. He is omnipotent. He is omniscient. We are taught, and we endeavor to believe that, above all our God is a God of infinite and abiding love and mercy. Yet, there are times when He does not show it, when we cannot see it, when it feels as if *no one* is there. There are times when we cannot seem to find Him.

We have all either experienced or observed the sufferings of pain in this world. For most of us, it is manageable. For some, it has been unfathomable. Tragedy seeks our attention each day and haunts our years. Its companion is a suffering that clouds our minds and pierces our hearts. It offers only despair or stoicism as its numbing resolution.

How is it possible that a God of infinite love, power and mercy could allow this endless procession of pain, suffering and tragedy in His world?

In my thirty years of practice as an attorney, it has been part of my profession to defend the innocent or to seek redress for those who suffer the wrongful acts of others. This question of pain and suffering has very often come to mind. Perhaps we cannot hold the Almighty accountable, but we are entitled to ask our questions and hope to understand who we are dealing with.

The purpose of this book is to explore and answer this question of pain and suffering. It is a question that is asked by each and every one of us sooner or later. As the answer to this quandary appears convincingly almost nowhere, we are left to rationalize it in various ways, if we care to go on believing in God. It is a question of profound consequence. Though many have considered it through the ages, seldom is there heard or offered a satisfying explanation. In times of tragedy, the words most often offered by the religious is that the will of God cannot always be known; that His will is just and merciful and must be accepted. Though comforting, these words are hardly illuminating.

Even worse, these vague answers may serve to plant the seeds of doubt and despair into the minds of some who consider this question. It is reasonable to assume that someone, some great thinker, by now, would have discerned and disseminated a solution capable of expressing the truth necessary to consider this problem in a more sophisticated way. As no 'Universal Truth' has been accepted or popularized in this area, it is safe to assume that either little confidence abides in any solution yet proffered or that there is no solution. Either way, the tepid result exposes a flaw in our concept of God.

Were this a minor flaw, trivial in nature, we could get on without concern, but this weakness is an epic and dreadful threat –a fundamental challenge to faith. It is meant to be attacked. If the attack be forestalled, then we are exposed and subject to great danger. The failure to answer this question must ultimately cause the house built upon sand to give way. The concept of a loving God who allows horrific tragedy to occur without end is tenuous.

The Bible gives no direct answer on this point. The charge is raised often enough, and nowhere more poignantly than in the Book of Job, but the question is more avoided than answered. The lack of resolution, therefore, arises from our most authentic source. Moreover, brilliant minds have considered it over the centuries without settling the issue. St. Augustine[1] addresses it, as do St. Thomas Aquinas[2] and C. S. Lewis,[3] but no consensus has developed. The opaque words of comfort offered in the face of tragedy are still the same.

More recently, both Pope Benedict and the Reverend Billy Graham have both been pointedly asked this question. Pope Benedict's response during a Good Friday question and answer session in 2011 was, "We do not have the answers."[4] Billy Graham's response to interviewer Larry King in 2006 was, "I don't know why."[5]

Even in the face of great tragedy, when we are most inclined to ponder the complexities of this paradox, our answers seem no better. In vain will we look for truth or understanding among all the discussions or discourses bred by the terrible destruction of the World Trade Center. Just the opposite was true. It was more common to hear men of faith, ministers and other religious leaders, despair and question than it was to hear cogent, faith-enriching elocution.

While watching a PBS documentary on the aftermath of that tragic event: Serious, somber interviews were conducted with religious leaders of all persuasions. I was caught off guard by how badly shaken the ministry seemed to be. Some were disillusioned; visibly distressed that there were no words to defend God in this event. In this fashion, one leader commented that this was "such an indifferent God." Another stated that "there is no good in this."[6] Similarly, a newspaper article entitled "Reflections on God and Men After A Disaster,"[7][7] surveyed eight religious leaders after another disaster. Six of the eight declared that they could not explain it, and two others detoured on tangents that offered no explanation. It is disappointing, yet wholly understandable. It is an intractable problem and a great dilemma, but it is a fatal disease and must be cured.

At this point, I must caution you that the answer to the question at hand is much larger and much different than you might expect. There are no magic words or concepts that will cure the ills of this world. Suffering will always exist. Nor will the concepts presented in this book enable the compassionate to soothe the sufferers any more than they are able to do now. Suffering is a process and must run its course. It is different for each individual, but it is at its core an emotional trauma. Concepts of the mind will not relieve the immediacy of the pain. They can, however, insulate us from and inoculate us against the perils of life we may later encounter. They can help us prepare to accept the pain with understanding when it comes and help us confront it in a healthier way after it passes us by.

One important attribute of this answer is that it will bring us to a greater understanding of who we are as human beings and encourage us to reach out to those in need. Verily, however, it will not eliminate distress or allow penetration of the veil of emotional hurt one may encounter in others. Though the truth could help them, it is unlikely they will often be ready to receive it.

On the positive side, truth and understanding have peculiar attributes that we often don't expect. The path towards truth often opens doors to even greater understanding than is sought. The light at the end of the tunnel may prove to be the very brightest light of all. For at the end of this journey, we will find God, Himself.

As all truth must end in God, I suppose this should not be so surprising. But how does one begin to explain that the answer to the question of why God allows pain and suffering in this world is because He loves you? It seems absurd. It is why our journey will necessarily traverse other destinations and consider concepts that are wholly intertwined with pain and suffering. If we are to understand why He allows it, then we must strive to understand His motives and challenges. We will, therefore, also discuss and analyze the relationship of pain and suffering to free will, creation, and the meaning of life. These other issues are directly related to why so much pain and suffering exists in God's world.

Eventually, these philosophical issues filter down to practical realities, however, and when this question intersects with daily life, the innocent are left to suffer.

Several years ago, a man sat before me seeking advice on how to respond to an impending divorce. The pain in his situation was palpable, and I asked him how it came to be. It all began, he explained, some years ago with the death of their five-month-old son due to Sudden Infant Death Syndrome, commonly known as SIDS. He simply came home one day... and his child was gone. His son had passed away all alone while his wife was in the other room. He explained that he and his wife had not been able to cope with it. They could not find a way to overcome their own pain and feelings of despair long enough to support each other deeply and soulfully in a manner that was sustainable. It just seemed to magnify the problems that already existed. I could not help but sense the anguish this man endured and the questions he must have asked – not only to lose a child so abruptly, but now a family, too.

The injustice and pain in losing a son in this way was not tempered by comfort and understanding but was compounded by depression and detachment. The original injustice was now multiplied. The incidence of divorce in cases like these, are well documented and predictable. There are those who argue that good can come of pain and suffering, but, that good seems to come all too seldom.

The truth is that he was a fine man. I had known him for some time on a professional basis and appreciated his many strong qualities and his integrity. He was involved in law enforcement and struck me as a particularly fair and thoughtful man. Though he worked to protect others, he was given no opportunity to protect his own. Without the hint of any emergency or any danger, his boy was silently taken, dying quietly in his sleep in the middle of his nap, leaving behind a grief that could not be healed.

Once again, this question comes to mind: *Where was God?* There were no answers then. As he sat in my office a few years later, the answers were no clearer. At some point in our conversation, I asked him if he blamed God for this tragedy and he admitted having an anger and resentment that he could not dispel. In fact, he was hardly able to relate to God at all anymore and had stopped practicing his faith.

Not quite sure how to comfort this man, I offered him my thoughts on God's role in this tragedy and His seeming indifference to what happened. I am not sure if I was of any help. It is unlikely there could ever be words so compelling that they would help relieve the chronic pain of such profound and recent loss. Words and thoughts at such a time are poor regulators of such deep emotion. The best I could hope to do was to plant some empathic seeds of understanding, and hope that he could find something that made sense.

Sadly, making sense of this world is sometimes an impossible task. When all is well, when peace or happiness prevails, then the world is a wonderful place full of magic and charm. No explanation seems necessary. Tragedy, however, gives us great pause. It can suddenly call into question everything we believe and test us beyond our capacity to understand, cope, or persevere. It is all the more difficult when it seems to be senseless - and we are frustrated by the injustice of it. Surely we can understand the tragedy of human error, or human failure, or malevolence, but how are we to understand the failure of God?

For here is the breaking point: Tragedy and suffering are the most dangerous and threatening to our sense of existence or existential well-being when we believe they are allowed by a loving God who has the power to stop them. For it is these tragedies, which seem the most unjust and frustrate our belief in and expectation of the Divine. They call into question not only faith, but the very existence of God. They bring us to the very edge of the universe and force us to face the eternal darkness and emptiness of the abyss.

This question first arose in me on a serious level when I was in high school. It is a question of the ages and required some attention at that stage, if only to determine where to fit it in my consciousness. I have been wrestling with the mystery ever since and have spent the last thirty years thinking about it from time to time.

At about the same time, I read G.K. Chesterton's <u>Orthodoxy</u>. Chesterton was a joyful and brilliant thinker whose life took a turn when he discovered the brave, 'new' world of Christianity and Catholicism in the midst of early 20th century London. He marveled how he felt he'd discovered an astonishing new world and was shocked to learn that it was merely the well-known and well-traveled place where he grew up. Once an agnostic, he began to eschew the philosophies of the day and learned to view the world from a 'new' perspective. Suddenly, everything seemed to make sense:

> "It was as if I had been blundering about since my birth with two huge and unmanageable machines, of different shapes and without apparent connection---the world and the Christian tradition. I had found this hole in the world: the fact that one must somehow find a way of loving the world without trusting it; somehow one must love the world without being worldly. I found this projecting feature of Christian theology, like a sort of hard spike, the dogmatic insistence that God was personal, and

had made a world separate from Himself. The spike of dogma fitted exactly into the hole in the world---it had evidently been meant to go there---and then the strange thing began to happen. When once these two parts of the two machines had come together, one after another, all the other parts fitted and fell in with an eerie exactitude. I could hear bolt after bolt over all the machinery falling into its place with a kind of click of relief. Having got one part right, all the other parts were repeating that rectitude, as clock after clock strikes noon. Instinct after instinct was answered by doctrine after doctrine."[8]

He was an astonishing writer, and I shared the exhilaration he felt as he expressed the basis of his faith. Though I agreed with him, I never felt I heard the clicks of the bolts of his machines lining up on the question of pain and suffering.

So, from a rather early age, this important issue felt unresolved. Seemingly unable to uncover any good clues about this mystery, I was ever more intrigued. A few years later, while in the Dominican Republic on an extended stay, I went to Mass one day and heard a sermon delivered in Spanish. Though I did not understand it thoroughly, I was able to follow that the topic was about freedom. Immediately, I knew that this word was the key to decoding the thoughts that were always present in the back of my mind.

My journey, exploring the problem of pain and suffering, has been slow and deliberate. My great advantage was I never had any question that God existed. I was brought up as a well-educated product of a liberal and Catholic education. I grew to love the Word of God and the Tradition of the Catholic Church in trying to understand and incorporate it. It is a rich tradition, and I was impressed both with its ability to pursue logic as far as it would go and its willingness to take an unshakeable leap of faith when necessary. As I felt not the slightest compunction to question the existence of God, even in the light of the problem of suffering, I felt no need to waste time or thought on the problem of His existence. My own experiences, personal and unique, in prayer and in life, convinced me that God existed. I was free of questioning it any further as I tackled the problem before me.

Moreover, as I was convinced there was a God, I was therefore absolutely convinced that there must be an answer to the mystery of suffering life in His presence, -for it was otherwise impossible to reconcile the two concepts. I was, then, over a long period of time, able to focus my mind solely on the proposition that there was a logical resolution to this question, and that I would not be swayed into accepting anything less.

My mind has filtered many ideas over the years, and it struck me at some point that this project might best be done unconventionally. I determined the best way to approach this quest was to turn inward. As traditional insights were either hidden from plain view or wholly lacking in substance, I thought it best to avoid them altogether. I committed to a fresh perspective and allowed my heart and mind to orbit this challenge over and over like two small satellites probing a great planet. The final solution proved elusive and exhausting, but like so many things with God charmingly simple too. It suggests that Truth can be pursued from any point, and when it is found it always has the same brilliance.

Once these ideas crystallized in my mind, as one working unit, I began to write this book from the many notes and clippings I had compiled over the years. It was only then that any research I had done for this book began in earnest. As many have written passionately, and some presciently, about this subject, I have been able to utilize some of their insights and ideas in the composition of this piece. Sometimes, this is happily unavoidable as their ideas are precisely mine (Happily, because I would prefer to believe that this points to some confirmation on larger issues of truth). Other times, their ideas, although astute, are given a new direction when they seem to fall short of the goal.

Whether my ideas contain essential truths, I cannot know. I do, however, find that they have satisfied me. Exploration of these truths can be a taxing and even treacherous proposition. We are painfully exposed and vulnerable in this world. The language of hope awaits us at the conclusion of our journey, but we must first soberly assess all aspects of pain and suffering.

It is plain to see that our desire to believe in God is constantly challenged by this world He has created. The realities of daily life and current events belie our hope and erode our faith. Due to these challenges, many have been lost to God. Despair creeps in and asks the question, "Can there be a God such as this?"

Without an answer to this question, the faith of some will ebb away. God's silence and inaccessibility imply indifference, leaving many to pursue more accessible gods: gods of materialism, pleasure, or instantaneous gratification, who at least are there when you call upon them. Gods who seem more logical and more suited to who we are as physical beings; gods who are not so mysterious, silent, and demanding; gods who do not frown upon conviviality.

Would it not be wiser to have created a world that rewards the right actions of its people? Would it not be wiser for God to show Himself occasionally? Should He not encourage us, lead us, and inspire us more tangibly? So often, we cry out to Him and we hear nothing.

If only I were God, I would answer. I would show myself and encourage my people. I would be a God of active, observant love, seeking to soften the rough edges and caress the broken spirits. With omnipotent power and inexhaustible love, I would balance the needs of individual freedom with the desires of faith. I would call to my people and interact with them frequently and tangibly. I would send them my angels. More than anything, I would mitigate or eliminate those emotions of fear from the world that are based on a pervasive sense of despair and hopelessness.

What kind of God gives us "everything" out of love, then watches some of us suffer catastrophe? Why does He create us and then threaten to burn us in hell?

If only I were God, I would create a more benevolent world. Yes, it would be a world of challenges, but it would be more interactive too. It would be a world of second chances. I would create a morally ordered, artful, and diverse universe where individuals could explore, develop, and thrive. It would be a world where they could look to me for help and have the hope that they would get it.

I would not, as the deists claim, create the universe and then abandon it. Nor would I threaten my people like a high school bully. Rather, I would nurture my children with affection and pursue a meaningful relationship with them. I would breathe new life into infants who die in their sleep and invest them with the instinct to seek the air that they need.

Would anyone choose much differently? It seems to make little sense that God did. Is it possible, after all, that there is no God?

Perhaps it makes more sense to believe that we created Him; that we simply need to believe in order to survive in a very difficult environment. Many have advanced such a position. Even worse, belief in God may reflect an immaturity that is an obstacle to our advancement as a civilization. Philosophers, like Friedrich Nietzsche, have taken that position.[2] Certainly many secularists today would agree.

In the final analysis there must be logic to our God. If there is no logic to Him or in Him, then He cannot exist; for no creature of His could ever find Him or know Him. Such a God would be an absurdity.

Our challenge, then, is to examine this world, this universe, this creation and explore how it was made. Specifically, we must further explore to what purpose it was made and whether its operation suits its purpose. For locked away in this strongbox are the answers to the questions we have about pain and suffering.

If we can answer these questions, and find an inexorable logic in them, then we cannot so easily dismiss our God. It is critical to our search, to first explicitly assume that God exists. We can logically answer all of the above questions by positing that there is no God, but that is not our quest. Our question is: Why would our God make such a world as this?

Our search and exploration, therefore, assumes the existence of God. Our task is to find logical, sensible, philosophical evidence of God in this creation of His.

Let us, therefore, start at the beginning…

Chapter One
GENESIS

"In the beginning, God created the heavens and the earth.
The earth was a formless wasteland and darkness covered
the abyss, while a mighty wind swept over the waters. Then
God said, "Let there be light," and there was light. God saw
how good the light was. God then separated the light from the
darkness. God called the light 'day' and the darkness He called
'night.' Thus, evening came, and morning followed – the first
day."
Genesis 1:1-5

PART I: THE GARDEN OF EDEN

Our first experience of God is as the Creator. If Genesis is accepted, then it is our first knowledge of Him as well. He created the Heavens and the Earth, the day and the night, and every creature in the sky, on the land, and in the water. Then, "God created man in His image, in the divine image he created him; male and female, He created them." Genesis 1:27

Our second image of God is as giver and provider. God gave to man dominion over all the creatures on Earth. He provided man all the fruits of the seed-bearing plants and trees. Next, He gave man the Garden of Eden and all of the peace, security, and serenity that God's garden implies. He gave man woman so he would not be alone.

Yet, according to Genesis, God gives even more. He freely invites man to eat of the Tree of Life, in the middle of the Garden of Eden. Presumably, man and woman are free to enjoy eternal life in the Garden of Eden with domain over every creature and every type of fruit and sustenance. It is a virtual heaven on Earth and everlasting as well.

Moreover, God gave His very presence, for it seems that He was known to visit the Garden of Eden and call for Adam. "When they heard the sound of the Lord God moving about in the garden at the breezy time of the day, the man and his wife hid themselves from the

Lord God among the trees of the garden. The Lord God then called to the man and asked him, 'Where are you?'" Genesis 3:8-9. There was an interaction with Adam in the way of a developing relationship.

To this point it is impossible to find any fault with the God of early Genesis. He is as we would like to see Him. He is awesome in His power and tender in His love. A creative force of love and mercy who provides everything for us. There is abundant love. There is the prospect of eternal peace and happiness. Moreover, the delightful overtures of a real, interactive, physical relationship are present. This is the God we would all choose to have. This is the God we long for and can understand. If only I were God, so would it always be.

This idyllic world of man, however, seems to teeter on the sharp precipice of one point: Man is forbidden to eat from the fruit of the Tree of Knowledge of Good and Bad. On this rule all is dependent: "The Lord God gave man this order: 'You are free to eat from any of the trees of the garden, except the Tree of Knowledge of Good and Bad. From that tree you shall not eat; the moment you eat from it you are surely doomed to die.'" Genesis 2:16-17. Without this tree, or this prohibition, man is poised to live forever in the lap of God.

But, as we all know, man is unable to abide the one rule set by God, and he is banished from Eden. Paradise is lost. Moreover, having tasted this fruit and having discerned the existence of this knowledge of good and evil, man is now also barred from the Tree of Life. "When He expelled the man, He settled him east of the Garden of Eden: and He stationed the cherubim and the fiery revolving sword, to guard the way to the Tree of Life." Genesis 3:24

What are we to make of all of this? In six days, according to Genesis, God created the universe and every creature in it. The purpose of all of this effort seems to be focused on the creation of man, a being made in the image and likeness of God. But then, in a matter of a few minutes, or an hour (or at most, an afternoon), God's plan seems to unravel. He becomes angry. He even acts as though He is a bit panic stricken. For the first time, we experience God as distant, aloof, mysterious, and hidden. Our loving, giving Creator has changed course. Disappointed in Adam and Eve, paradise is sealed and guarded. Man is now destined to suffer and struggle on his own. God is no longer a friend among us, but a mysterious and distant power.

As a result, the idyllic world of Genesis is not the world of our experience. Our world is fraught with disappointment, danger, and death. There are many great obstacles to the joy that we seek. It is not, after all, so easy to understand this God of ours.

We are about to pursue a great journey of understanding. The God of Genesis has banished us from Eden, and we are left to fend for ourselves. We are about to embark upon a long road to help us explain why the children of God are subjected to the unrelenting occurrence of pain and suffering.

Genesis is the beginning of that journey. The very first words of the very first book in the Bible, one of the oldest and most important books ever written, are perhaps the most significant words in all of literature. The very first stories of Genesis describe creation and the instance of pain and suffering. So, from the earliest points in human civilization, we are confronted with the most fundamental concepts of human life. Indeed, we are confronted with the very meaning of life. We are asked two fundamental questions: What is our relationship to God, and why are we allowed to suffer? The answers are tightly wrapped up in the mystery of creation and its relationship to pain and suffering. These two ideas, the mystery of creation and the mystery of pain and suffering, are the seminal points in the Genesis narrative, and the connection between them is pivotal. Genesis challenges us to understand this connection. To understand the relationship between the mysteries of creation and pain and suffering, is to understand everything. We will, therefore, explore these two concepts in order to understand the predicament of our vulnerability – our susceptibility to pain and suffering as children of God.

PART II: GENESIS REWRITTEN

Genesis declares that God is our Creator and recognizes the plight of our suffering. We have addressed these ideas in a spiritual way ever since. In the beginning, without scientific proof or even a rudimentary understanding of science at all, we have accepted, in faith, that God is our Creator. Without understanding the cause of pain and suffering, we have grown in faith to accept it as part of God's plan.

Over the centuries, a deeper understanding of our physical surroundings grew into the study of science and led us to a more enlightened and comprehensive vision of the physical universe and of creation. As we pursue our task and seek to solve the dilemma of pain and suffering, we will realize that it is, in fact, a creation problem. As we reconsider the questions presented in Genesis, we shall begin to see that, despite all of their differences, science and spirituality converge at the very point of creation.

It is at this precise point that the tale of how and why the universe was created began to be told. The Genesis story addresses these two questions: the how and the why. Through science and spirituality, through reason and faith, humanity has long explored the depths of these very complex issues.

As we begin to address how the universe was created, we must and should look to science. For those who believe there is a God, or for those who are at least willing to consider the possibility, whatever science can tell us about the method of creation must shed light on the purpose of creation. If there is a God, He chose to create this universe in the one way in which it was created. Assuming we can understand how He created it, then we are left with one of two possibilities: Either He created it with some purpose in mind, or He did not (I would assert this point is true, even if He determined to create us in some random fashion or even if He determined to create us in a way that we can never discover). If He did not create the universe with any purpose in mind, then it seems we are dealing with a rather silly deity. If there was a purpose to creation, then the manner and method of creation ought to shed some light on its purpose and the discoveries of science are extremely important and relevant to our analysis.

For a great part of our history, we have presumed to understand the goal of creation and have arrogantly tended to impose that view on our beliefs about the method of creation. And so, we came to believe that the sun revolved around the earth; that the universe is only thousands of years old; that evolution is improbable, and the laws of physics produce a mechanistic and predictable universe. Over time, we have been forced to admit the earth is not the center of the universe; the universe is over 13 billion years old; evolution is highly probable; and uncertainty is intrinsic to the laws of physics.

Our past presumptions about the intent of creation clouded our thinking and became obstacles to scientific truth. It is plain to see that our ideas about the purpose of creation should not be the basis for understanding the method of creation. Rather, just the opposite should occur. As we are further able to unravel the scientific mysteries of creation, we should carefully incorporate those discoveries into a spiritual consideration of the purpose of creation. We should not rely so heavily on our subjective understanding of God's intent in order to understand His method. Rather, we should rely on our objective understanding of His method, in order to more faithfully and respectfully consider His purpose.

For this reason, we will need some basic understanding of the perspective and sensibilities of science and the scientific method. Such an understanding will more fully equip us to pursue the spiritual depths of the purpose of God's creation. It will also help us understand how pain and suffering are related to that purpose. If we can understand the scientific truth of creation, we can then better understand why God created us and what He intends for us. Science does not speak to the philosophy of the question of pain and suffering, but it does speak to the issue and circumstances of creation. As it does so, we must listen to the gentle whispers of meaning and intent.

As is well known, the scientific community tells a different creation story then that presented in Genesis. Science believes that the universe began with the Big Bang some 13.7 billion years ago. From that point forward, a physical process unfolded that resulted in the development of conscious life: The pinnacle and perhaps the goal of creation. This metamorphosis crystallized through a series of dynamic phenomenon, including the hyperinflation of the universe and the formation of stars, galaxies, and planets. Though some aspects of this theory are still unresolved, few, if any, serious scientists dispute the basic principles of the Big Bang.

Science today continues vigorously to pursue some of the most incomprehensible aspects of this theory. In particular, it is probing its precursor: The principles or cause that may have ignited the Big Bang. One leading hypothesis, in that regard, is called string theory, a complex model that reduces the most basic elements in the universe to ultra-microscopic vibrating strings and involves as many as eleven different dimensions. Though it is far from proven, string theory is just one example of the dynamic vitality of scientific inquiry and investigation that has richly improved human life.

Through publication of hypotheses, transparency of testing, mathematical proofs, and the rigorous public discourse within the scientific community, we are well able to rely on their discoveries and hard pressed to deny their findings. The Big Bang theory may be incomplete on some levels, but it is truly a remarkable description of creation in its own right, meticulously unraveled and reviewed over a long period of time by some of history's most brilliant scientists. A working knowledge of its principles can only enhance the appreciation of the journey that we are about to begin. A brief summary of its principles is, therefore, in order.

As a starting point, let us imagine that a modern scientist, with a lyrical bent, rewrote Genesis today. It may look something like this:

In the beginning, the four known forces of the universe were one and all the power, mass, space/time, and energy of the universe were constrained to a point inconceivably small. 13.7 billion years ago, the unity was broken, and the primeval atom relinquished its hold on the fury within.

Within 1 billionth of a second, a bubble smaller and hotter than can be seen or imagined comprises the whole universe. The force of gravity breaks free from the other 3. The universe expands and the unimaginable heat dissipates into the expansion. Thus ends the first phase of the creation of the universe.

Within one second of its being, with the laws of physics still unsettled, hyperinflation expands the borders of the universe faster than the speed of light, carrying an equal share of its energy and heat uniformly to all distant points. All four known forces of the universe: Gravity, Electro-magnetic, Strong Nuclear

& Weak Nuclear, are now divided. The 2nd phase of the history of the universe is complete.

Within three minutes, the temperature of the universe has cooled to one billion degrees Fahrenheit. Hydrogen atoms are formed, and helium arises from hydrogen fusion. Thus ends the 3rd phase.

Within 380,000 years, light emerges from the clouded maelstrom and extends into the expanding universe. The light of creation races into the darkness. Thus ends the 4th phase of the history of the universe.

Upon the elapse of one billion years, massive stars form. Hot enough to create nitrogen, oxygen, and carbon within their fiery furnaces, their deaths give rise to elemental clouds of dust and matter. Thus ends the fifth phase of creation.

Upon the elapse of nine billion years, gravity coalesces the dust and debris into the stars, planets, and moons. The universe continues to expand, the sixth phase.

Upon the dawn of the present age, the universe is 93 billion light years across and encompasses 2 trillion galaxies. On the outer edge of one such galaxy, on the third planet from the sun, primordial life emerges from an environment rich with hydrogen, oxygen, nitrogen, and carbon. Simple life evolves into complex life forms, and 150,000 years ago, a species called homo-sapiens arrive. Man evolves.

Thus, the heavens and the earth and all their array were completed to the present day.[1]

Genesis Rewritten clearly shows the Bible and science are speaking different languages, not to mention, addressing different audiences. Genesis addresses the scientific, but especially the spiritual questions of early man. 21st century science is a sophisticated approach to questions arising from the study of the physical universe. It is appropriately disinterested in spiritual, and especially religious, affairs. Genesis sets the tone for a relationship with God, that is developed over time, as related in the Bible. Genesis Rewritten neither accepts nor acknowledges God. In truth, it does not preclude Him either, but it is not part of the scientific mission to consider Him. Genesis is revelation and a transcendental path to the meaning of life. Science is measurement, discovery, proof, and an intimate understanding of our surroundings. It is a well-tested, well-developed discipline, fully capable of discovering truth.

Ultimately, the analysis of these two differing viewpoints does not mean that they must be at cross-purposes. They both pursue truth. The difficulty comes when one side insists on its own, incomplete view of truth and rejects other truth. The difficulty comes from territorial closed-mindedness, from confusing long accepted ideas with truth, and from stubbornly refusing to consider a greater truth. Though it is beyond our scope to encounter the great depth and complexity of the science of creation - from classical physics to quantum mechanics, from genetics to evolution, from special relativity to string theory, we would be unequipped to consider the totality of our circumstances if we did not consider and appreciate the relevance of scientific discovery.

If we are to pursue truth, we must be aware of whatever truth science unveils. Truth incorporates all aspects of life and explains all mysteries. It can be pursued from any source and any direction. Scientific truth is part of who we are and part of the spiritual journey we are on. It is a product of the gift of life, bestowed by the Creator and meant for us to have.

PART III: THE MIRACLE OF CREATION

As we more deeply consider scientific principles, we necessarily have a greater understanding of the majesty of God. Such an understanding can only serve to deepen our relationship with God and clarify it in the light of a more honest perspective. It will more successfully allow us to seek the answers for the questions we ask.

Thus, the first question that comes to mind is what happened at the moment of creation?

The spiritual believe that God created the universe; it was simply an act of His will. They will never have actual knowledge of this, but they do not care. It is what they believe in faith, for a host of reasons.

Science, on the other hand, is deeply interested in what happened at the moment of creation. It is focused and intent on discovering creation's cause. The physics community, along with the cosmologists, has devoted vast energy and dedication to solving this problem. Like the spiritualists, scientists may be beginning to realize that they may never know.

As we have seen from Genesis Rewritten, science has revealed a detailed and intricate portrait of creation. It has gone back in time to a billionth of a second after the Big Bang. But before that, there is silence. It is not the silence of a lack of effort or lack of ideas, or speculation or testing, but the silence of results.

The discoveries described in Genesis Rewritten have left scientists with one enormous problem: The science and the mathematical equations of the Big Bang show unequivocally that the existence of life in this, or any universe, created by a big bang is one incredible long shot. Michael Turner astrophysicist at the University of Chicago likens it to an amazing dart toss. *"The precision is as if one could throw a dart across the entire universe and hit a bulls-eye one millimeter in diameter on the other side," says Turner.*[2]

Statistically speaking, there is no chance that we should be here. But we are. It is an anomaly of mind-blowing proportions. The analysis of the existence of life, despite these overwhelming odds, is referred to as the Anthropic Principle. We will discuss this principle in more detail later in this chapter. For now, suffice it to say that it helps us to understand one thing. Despite all of the remarkable advancements of science, and of the science of creation in particular, there are still gaping holes in our knowledge.

The significance of the Anthropic Principle is that it has disconcerted the scientific community and compelled them to look beyond the Big Bang to answer the call of this statistical anomaly. The essence of the problem is that currently, Big Bang theory forces scientists to accept certain, precise, given numbers for the values of some forces and relationships in the universe in order for life to exist. These numbers, sometimes called constants, are unexplained by science, but without them life never materializes.

The point of fact is that the constants are real, and they are inexplicably set at the precise values that allow life to occur. Slightly different values would produce no life, yet it is far more likely that a universe with different values would have arisen.

Science, however, does not accept the inexplicable. Its mission is to explain everything there is to know about physical reality. It is not surprising, therefore, that science is diligently seeking an answer to the questions raised by the Anthropic Principle. It is currently investigating numerous complex models, which could account for the statistically slim chance of our existence. These complex models are born of hypotheses based on string theory, singularities (like black holes), inflation theory, and other sources. What they all have in common is this universe must have been created as part of a process or a cycle, and not as a one-time event.

In other words, our universe could be one of many universes. In effect, we may be one universe out of a multiverse of perhaps billions or trillions of universes. We may have evolved in our peculiar universe due to differing vibrations of ultra-microscopic strings in different dimensions; we may have evolved as the result of a collision between two other universes; we may simply have been born of a black hole in another universe. Any of these ongoing cycles would produce vast numbers of universes – all different from our own – and would thereby account for the statistical anomaly that is found in the life-producing universe we call our own. If there are enough other universes, then eventually one like ours, with the constants and values necessary to sustain life, would be born.

This is rather logical speculation on the part of science. If the odds for life cannot be accounted for, then it makes sense to improve the odds. There are, however, two important problems with this line of thinking. First, it is completely speculative. No proof has been found for any of these other universes. Even worse, it is unlikely that proof of another universe could ever be found. How does science get beyond its own physical reality in this universe to test for another universe? Even if it makes logical sense, how can it be tested directly? Though the mathematical models of these hypotheses are found to be intriguing by scientists, and though they may even be useful in theorizing about our own universe, it is difficult to conceive how they could ever be relied upon to prove what they assert.

Moreover, these hypotheses do not really get to the heart of the problem. Even were we to assume that there is a multiverse, full of enough universes to guarantee the statistical inevitability of the life we find in our universe, how do we explain where that process all started? What caused the first Big Bang? How did the cycle begin? Where did the original energy come from? Should we accept, as given, that this energy always existed? If we do that, why don't we just accept the constants?

Without going any deeper into these issues now, we can see that the explanation of the creation of the universe may not be entirely possible. Yet, it is this very problem which I believe to be central to the dilemma of pain and suffering, which we will soon begin to explore.

PART IV: MODERN SCIENCE

Let us take one last departure into the world of science before we begin, in earnest, a direct explanation of the questions and issues to be addressed by this book. An overview of modern science and the intuition of its scientists will be important as a foundation of our understanding of the creation problem and its connection to pain and suffering.

The question has often been asked by philosophers and by most every common man and woman: Why did God make the world the way He did? (The implication being that God could have made it a little better!) One famous mathematician and philosopher who thought about this question was Gottfried Wilhelm Liebniz. He was a famously brilliant man and, among other things, invented the mathematical principles of calculus in Germany just as Isaac Newton was doing so in England. Liebniz concluded that this was the best possible world that God could create.[3] This conclusion was famously ridiculed by the derisive wit of Voltaire, a popular French philosopher and social critic: "What then must the others be like?" he retorted.[4]

Though intending later to rejoin this debate, let us spend a few minutes recalling and exploring what modern science knows and understands today about what God did create. In so doing, we shall also briefly consider, with some help from leading authors and physicists, the impact of scientific discovery and innovation on scientists themselves and the world in which they live.

Modern science begins with Isaac Newton and his ability to describe and calculate the larger scale forces of nature, in particular gravity and motion. From the 17th century to the 20th, his model of the universe, classical physics, was relied upon to explain the relationships of physical bodies and forces. Newton was an incredible genius, who observed the visible forces of nature and developed the means to calculate and predict them to a degree of accuracy far exceeding the need of his times.

He postulated, as you may recall, the three laws of motion: First, that an object in motion (or at rest) continues to remain so unless an external force is applied to it; Second, that any change of motion is proportional to the force applied; and Third, that for every action there is an equal and opposite reaction.

About gravity, Newton concluded that, "Every particle of matter in the universe attracts every other particle with a force that is directly proportional to the product of their masses and inversely proportional to the square of the distance between them."[5] He realized that this force applied to the planets and stars, just as it did to objects on the earth. This realization largely resolved all outstanding issues of his day regarding planetary movements.

His discoveries inevitably influenced the views of many in philosophy and religion. As some were already visualizing the universe as a machine, Newton now delivered the operating instructions. The physical forces of the universe, the laws of Nature, could be deconstructed and understood. Newton gave impetus to the preeminence of human rationality in the Age of Enlightenment.

Theism, the idea of an interventionist God, was now confronted with a more mechanistic viewpoint of the universe, which supported the philosophies of rationalism and materialism. These new theories elevated the provenance of physical processes and reason. These new philosophies advocated the idea that physical matter, Natural Law, and the human intellect capable of discerning them, could explain all there was in the universe.

With Newton, science had taken a great leap forward. However, even Newton readily admitted he did not understand how the force of gravity worked. He could measure it, but he couldn't explain it. Even so, his models were highly accurate and reliable, and they were found useful well through the end of the 19th century.

At the beginning of the 20th century, however, scientists had discovered inconsistencies with the classical physics of Newton, particularly with regard to the nature of light and electromagnetism. These issues piqued the curiosity of Albert Einstein, an otherwise unknown patent clerk living in Switzerland. With incredible insight, fortitude, and genius, he devised a completely new system, which successfully addressed the inconsistencies of the Newtonian classical model.[6]

Initially, this new insight had to do with the speed of light and the relativity of motion and was developed into the theory of special relativity. Among other things, Einstein single-handedly deduced that the speed of light was the absolute speed attainable in the universe. He set forth that the speed of light never changes. It never slows down or stops, and it moves at light speed irrespective of the speed or movement of any other object. In other words, whether one was standing still on the sidewalk as a beam of light approached him or whether one was in a rocket ship speeding away from that same beam of light, the rate of speed at which the speed of light would catch up to this individual is identical.

As part of this same theory, Einstein determined that all other motion in the universe is relative. Except for light, the concept of motion is meaningless without an object of comparison. One would be completely unaware of motion unless there were other stationary objects in view. It explains the phenomenon encountered when one is sitting in a train, which is parked next to another train. As one of the trains begins to move, it can be difficult, at first, for the passenger to determine if the one moving is the one in which he is sitting. Only when other objects come into view will the passenger realize which train is moving. Einstein also discovered that the speed of an object affects the lapse of time. The faster one moves, the slower time elapses. Though this is not detectible in everyday life, it would be obvious at very great speeds. If one were to attain the speed of light, no time would elapse at all.

The theory of special relativity caused a sensation in the scientific community. It, in turn, led to a whole new theory of gravity, again by Einstein, a few short years later. By 1919, this new theory, called the theory of general relativity, had been proven in experiments done by his colleagues. According to Harvard professor and physicist, Brian Greene, Einstein was the first to actually understand and explain what gravity is: "Gravity, according to Einstein, is the warping of space and time"[7] and, ". . .the mere presence of an object with mass causes space to respond by warping."[8]

In describing Einstein's new theory, Professor Greene chooses a word that is repeatedly heard from scientists – elegance. *"Most people who study general relativity are captivated by its aesthetic elegance. By replacing the cold, mechanistic Newtonian view of space, time, and gravity with a dynamic and geometric description involving curved spacetime, Einstein wove gravity into the basic fabric of the universe. Rather than being imposed as an additional structure, gravity becomes part and parcel of the universe at its most fundamental level. Breathing life into space and time by allowing them to curve, warp, and ripple results in what we commonly refer to as gravity."[9]*

Though Einstein had not yet realized it, the seeds of the Big Bang and quantum mechanics were also imbedded in his theory of general relativity. Though resisted by Einstein at first, these concepts were rather quickly discovered by the scientific community. A new scientific revolution was revealed. Einstein's equations of general relativity, when applied to the universe as a whole, explicitly showed that the universe was either expanding or shrinking.[10] The Big Bang was discovered in the idea, verified by Edwin Hubble in the 1920s, that the universe was expanding. The inescapable conclusion, verified by scientists in the ensuing decades, being that it was ever smaller in the past.

This mission, called science, was suddenly on a new path. With the principles of motion and gravity on larger scales now better understood, the physics of smaller and smaller particles became more and more important. What goes on at microscopic levels of the universe? What happened when the universe itself was microscopic at the time of the Big Bang? Modern science now turned its attention to quantum mechanics.

Quantum mechanics, the study of the relationship of particles and forces on a microscopic level, was given great impetus by the discovery of the 'uncertainty principle' by German physicist, Werner Heisenberg in 1927. Professor Greene tells us that "Heisenberg's uncertainty principle asserts that a...frantic shifting back and forth of energy and momentum is occurring perpetually in the universe on microscopic distance and time intervals."[11] It is occurring such that "at a microscopic level *you cannot possibly know both of these features* (the position and the velocity of a particle) *with total precision.*"[12] In fact, if you were to capture a single electron in a big, solid box and then slowly crush the sides to pinpoint its position with ever greater precision, you would find the electron getting more and more frantic."[13]

The upshot is that on very small, microscopic levels, precise measurements and predictions cannot be made. The precise and predictable world of Newtonian classical physics fades into a more and more chaotic substructure as the smallest particles of the universe are probed. A level of uncertainty is built into the universe and physics must now account for, and measure in, probabilities. Moreover, the elemental nature of particles has become smaller and more complex. When once we talked of neutrons and electrons, science has now also discovered quarks and force particles called gluons, photons, bosons, and gravitons. When once we talked of particles and waves, science now realizes that they are not so distinct. Particles can have wave-like properties and vice versa. In other words, not only is the measurement of energy and matter relative, as demonstrated by Einstein's famous equation $E = mc2$, but in some respects, they share the same structure.

PART V: SCIENTIFIC INTUITION

The philosophical and scientific principles of order, established in Newton's time, were now inadequate. This is never easy to accept. Every age has its foundational set of core values. To begin to comprehend that they are false, or misleading, can cause personal doubt and social anxiety.

Even Einstein, as brilliant a visionary as there ever was in science, fell prey to his own preconceived spiritual notions. A famous story, routinely told, describes Einstein's frustration with the theory of quantum physics and highlights the dichotomy in the scientific community as to the implications of scientific theory on the existence of God. Einstein struggled to reconcile the concepts of quantum mechanics with his personal view of God. Now, it must be said that his views on God are somewhat ambiguous and disputed to this day, but like many scientists, he had developed a certain innate, intuitive view of the universe based on his experiences grappling with the intricacies of physics, as well as his experiences of life. Ultimately, these views affect the analysis of many scientists, as these impressions will come to influence what path, in all the universe, they would choose to consider when solving a particular scientific problem. Based on his implicit understandings and beliefs, Einstein could not accept the random and arbitrary nature underlying quantum physics. Einstein famously dismissed this concept by asserting "God does not play dice with the universe." Even he eventually came to admit he was wrong about the nature of quantum physics, but his remark demonstrates two ideas that we will return to repeatedly in our spiritual quest.

First, it is important to accept truth wherever we find it, no matter how inconvenient. Second, we will not necessarily find God where we wish Him to be, but rather that we must learn to look for Him where He is. It is not our experiences that are wrong. It is not our scientific discoveries that are wrong. It is our understanding and our inability to integrate what we know, experience, and would like to believe that is inadequate.

Einstein's theories helped to more accurately explain the nature of motion and gravity but were still primarily focused on the larger objects of classical physics. Quantum mechanics recognized an entirely different and radical approach to small objects was necessary. Science has been attempting to reconcile the differences between classical physics and quantum mechanics ever since. Of the four known forces of the universe (strong nuclear, electromagnetic, weak nuclear, and gravity), quantum physics has successfully integrated three of them into one mathematical model. Einstein's theory of gravity, however, has escaped this effort so far.

This goal of integration is central to the heart and soul of science, which desires to explain all of physical reality in one grand theory. Einstein called it the Grand Unification Theory, and he pursued it without success until the end of his life.

In large part due to the inability of science to understand and integrate all four of these known forces into one grand equation, string theory was born. Of all the theories mentioned so far, it is the most theoretical and speculative – a work in progress. Once again, we turn to Professor Greene, "According to string theory, the elementary ingredients of the universe are not point particles. Rather they are tiny, one-dimensional filaments somewhat like infinitely thin rubber bands vibrating to and fro[14]...Just as the different vibrational patterns of a violin string give rise to different musical notes, *the different vibrational patterns of a fundamental string give rise to different masses and force changes.*"[15]

Though far from proven and fantastically complex, string theory is important to scientists for two reasons: First, and most importantly, it has the potential to provide a unified framework for all of the properties and laws of physics. If proven, it would bring together the four known forces of the universe into one working equation capable of explaining everything that is in the universe. Additionally, it would do so without relying on some of the arbitrary and unexplained features present in the standard model of physics. Second, to many of the scientists working on this idea, it just feels right. Professor Greene relays the following observation by another physicist, Michael Green, "The moment you encounter string theory and realize that almost all of the major developments in physics over the last hundred years emerge with such elegance – from such a simple starting point, you realize that this incredibly compelling theory is in a class of its own."[16]

As alluded to earlier, a number of other competing hypotheses are also being proposed and studied to help explain the unresolved issues of quantum mechanics relative to the Big Bang theory. Even today, major experiments are being undertaken to confirm certain aspects of these hypotheses. It remains unclear when, and if, the next big leap forward, capable of changing our worldview, will come.

The need for these evolving theories is twofold: One is to help the continuing development of the Big Bang theory, and the other is to reconcile subatomic science with our understanding of the world at large. Though for our purposes, there is no need to reach a deeper understanding of scientific principles, an interesting byproduct emerges from such a study, which is relevant to our cause.

As one reads the current texts concerning and explaining scientific discovery, one cannot help but notice frequent references to the elegance, economy, beauty, symmetry, and depth encountered by scientists in their work. Time and again these texts make plain that scientists emerge from their pursuits with an emotional reaction to this elegance, ingenuity, and power inherent in their discoveries and equations. It reassures them that they have discovered truth and often leads them or others to conjecture about the metaphysical significance of those discoveries. We have seen this in Newton's age, and it continues to the present day. This interplay between scientific discovery and philosophical insight has been a singular thread since the inception of serious scientific achievement.

This sense of awe, referred to by modern scientists and inspired by their discoveries, is sometimes at odds with the scientific mission. It can sometimes encroach upon the usual scientific indifference to religious ideas and promote in some scientists the sense of awe believers feel about the Almighty. Accordingly, some scientists are profoundly struck by these incredible features, which seem to underlie all of science. Some of them, though certainly not all, consider these features to be both extraordinarily beautiful and highly meaningful.

Normally, these elegant features are found hidden by scientists within the equations of the discoveries they are pursuing. Sometimes, however, they are evident in the very discovery itself, affording even the layman, with an illustration of the currents of philosophy that swirl around and beneath the otherwise innocuous approach to scientific questions.

One such discovery, noted earlier, is known as the Anthropic Principle. Deep within an understanding of the scientific principles behind Genesis Rewritten is the realization that the odds against our existence are incredibly long. As scientists have scrupulously studied every aspect of the Big Bang theory, they have come to realize that there are a number of chance circumstances so incredibly fortuitous that we could not have come into existence if they were otherwise.

These circumstances have come to be known as the Anthropic Principle - chance occurrences so arbitrary, so necessary, and so extraordinary that it colors the whole process of creation of life as orchestrated and manipulated. In fact, many scientists who have studied these principles seem to regard these principles as a "fix;" the arbitrary process of creation must have been designed to create life.

The Anthropic Principle contends that the universe was brought into existence intentionally, for the sake of producing mankind. All physicists are aware of these principles. Some believe they are an indication of divine intervention; others argue that they are simply not yet explained. This idea first came to the attention of the scientific community when Fred Hoyle, a 20th century British astronomer, undertook the study of the formation of carbon, a necessary element for life, which is produced within stars. He famously concluded that:

> "A commonsense interpretation of the facts suggests that a superintendent has monkeyed with the physics, as well as chemistry and biology, and that there are no blind forces worth speaking about in nature. I do not believe that any physicist who examined the evidence could fail to draw the inference that the laws of nuclear physics have been deliberately designed with regard to the consequences they produce within stars."[12]

The brilliant theoretical physicist and cosmologist Stephen Hawking explains this further:

> "If the electric charge of the electron had been only slightly different, stars would have been unable to burn hydrogen and helium, or else they would not have exploded...It seems clear that there are relatively few ranges of values for the numbers (for the constants) that would allow for development of any form of intelligent life. Most sets of values would give rise to universes

29

that, although they might be very beautiful, would contain no one able to wonder at that beauty."[18]

Two further examples help quantify the level of coincidence and contrivance that Hoyle and Hawking were talking about. High energy physicist Steven Weinberg points out that, "Life as we know it would be impossible if any one of several physical quantities had slightly different values." He goes on to describe how a beryllium isotope, having the minuscule half-life of 1/10,000th of a trillionth of a second, must find and absorb a helium nucleus in that split of time before decaying. This occurs only because of a totally unexpected, exquisitely precise, energy match between the two nuclei. If this did not occur, there would be none of the heavier elements. Our universe would be composed of only hydrogen and helium.[19]

Roger Penrose, the Rouse Ball Professor of Mathematics at the University of Oxford, discovered that the likelihood of the universe having usable energy (low entropy) at the creation is even more astounding:

> *"...namely, an accuracy of one part out of ten to the power of ten to the power of 123. This is an extraordinary figure. One could not possibly even write the number down in full, in our ordinary denary (power of ten) notation: it would be one followed by ten to the power of 123 successive zeros!" That is a million billion billion billion billion billion billion billion billion billion billion billion billion billion zeros. Penrose continues, "Even if we were to write a zero on each separate proton and on each separate neutron in the entire universe – and we could throw in all the other particles for good measure -- we should fall far short of writing down the figure needed."*[20]

There are commonly thought to be fifteen or more other examples of similar magnitude. These anomalies have yet to be formally explained by secular science and, to say the least, they certainly bring a sobering disposition to the scientific analysis of creation. However, the scientific study of creation theory is far more complex than the obvious implication of a Creator that the Anthropic Principle brings to the table. Though the very idea of unexplained and arbitrarily set realities, going back to the beginning of time, are extremely discomforting to scientists, we must be careful to guard against facile oversimplification in considering this concept. For it is not my intent to argue that these principles somehow prove the existence of God. Other scientific theories, if similarly allowed to persist in oversimplification, would seem to argue against the theory of the existence of God. Rather, it is my intent to suggest that facts are facts, wherever we find them, and we should learn to look at them with a clear eye that can open the mind to full understanding.

As discussed earlier, the significance of the Anthropic Principle is it has led science to acknowledge that the odds against our existence are beyond comprehension. Accordingly, in a logical, though highly speculative, manner, they are hypothesizing models that include an extraordinary number of universes in order to reduce those odds to a range where our existence becomes more probable. It is not my intent to disparage this effort, for it seems a prudent inquiry and is quite possibly correct, nor is it my intent to elevate the Anthropic Principle into a proof of God. It is no such thing. Other explanations are possible, and science is, in fact, pursuing them.

Despite the great wealth of features like elegance, economy, depth, and symmetry uncovered in scientific endeavor and suggestive of a divine or supernatural source, there is a flip side of equal note. For many in science, the mission of science remains the complete explanation of the universe without reference to God. As science endeavors to uncover all there is to know about creation, it pursues various theories where there seems to be no obvious reason for the necessity of a creator. In fact, the development of the "no boundaries" theory by the great physicist, Stephen Hawking, makes the case that the universe could have started itself.

This intriguing idea is far too complex to consider here, but it is worth reviewing the comments of Carl Sagan, a famous cosmologist, as to the implications he found in Hawking's hypothesis. In his foreword to Stephen Hawking's book, <u>A Brief History of Time</u>, he had this to say:

> *"This is also a book about God...or perhaps about the absence of God. The word God fills these pages. Hawking*

embarks on a quest to answer Einstein's famous question about whether God had any choice in creating the universe. Hawking is attempting, as he explicitly states, to understand the mind of God. And this makes all the more unexpected the conclusion of the effort, at least so far: a universe with no edge in space, no beginning or end in time, and nothing for a Creator to do.[21]

Though far from proven, this theory and others like it confront the possibility that we are fortuitous byproducts of a wholly self-contained physical process, a process without any special significance until the recent acquisition of consciousness by humanity. Thus, despite the awe-inspiring design uncovered in so many areas of scientific inquiry, the mission of science to explore all aspects of the physical world can lead to a contrary view. Indeed, it is only right that science should pursue its hypotheses and ideas, wherever they lead. Science is, in fact, on a grand mission to discover truth, and it should pursue it fully and objectively.

Specifically, this mission seeks to integrate all of the laws of physics in one grand mathematical equation. The pursuit of this grand equation is the holy grail of the physics community. Its discovery would, in theory, be able to explain all that happens in the physical universe. It has been pursued vigorously and creatively with great intellectual vitality and determination since Einstein's discoveries of the Theories of Special Relativity and General Relativity. Scientists now refer to it as the Theory of Everything. If discovered, it would precisely explain how every force of nature in the universe works and how they interact with each other on every level. It would explain everything. As the brilliant physicist, Stephen Hawking boldly points out, it could even open up a window to the mind of God:

"However, if we do discover a complete theory, it should in time be understandable in broad principle by everyone, not just a few scientists. Then we shall all, philosophers, scientists, and just ordinary people, be able to take part in the discussion of the question of why it is that we and the universe exist. If we find the answer to that, it would be the ultimate triumph of human reason – for then we would know the mind of God."[22]

Whether this lofty goal is attainable is an open question. At the conclusion of his work The Elegant Universe, Professor Greene comments on the prospects of the efforts of science in that regard:

"String theory offers an improvement by showing how such infinite extremes (in prior theories) might be avoided; nevertheless, no one has any insight on the question of how things actually did begin. In fact, our ignorance persists on an even higher plane: We don't know whether the question of determining the initial conditions is one that is even sensible to ask or whether...it is a question that lies forever beyond the grasp of any theory."[23]

"Maybe we will have to accept that certain features of the universe are the way they are because of happenstance, accident or divine choice...indeed, the possibility that there are limits to scientific explanation, in the broad way we have stated it, is an issue that may never be resolved."[24]

Professor Paul Davies, physicist, well-known author and Templeton award winner echoes these thoughts in his book The Mind of God:

"Sooner or later we all have to accept something as given, whether it is God, or logic, or a set of laws, or some other foundation for existence. Thus 'ultimate' questions will always lie beyond the scope of empirical science as it is usually defined. So, does this mean that the really deep questions of existence are unanswerable? I notice, on perusing the list of my chapter and section titles, that an awful lot of them are questions. At first I thought this was stylistic ineptitude, but I now realize that it reflects my instinctive belief that it is probably impossible for poor, old Homo sapiens to 'get to the bottom of it all.' Probably there must always be some 'mystery at the end of the universe.' But it seems worth pursuing the path of rational inquiry to its limit. Even a proof that the chain of inference is incompletable would be worth knowing. As we shall see, something of that sort has already been demonstrated in mathematics."[25]

As should be plain by now, even from this cursory review of modern science, there is astounding complexity at the heart of creation and its fundamental principles. For the purposes of this book, it is not of critical importance that we thoroughly understand the core principles of physics, but that we realize that there are fundamental truths discovered by science. Recognition of these truths may require that we reconsider our understanding of God and the way He operates in our universe. Quantum mechanics is but one example of that proposition: Changing our view of the universe from controlled and mechanistic to free flowing and undetermined. Even more importantly, the ideas put forth by Greene and Davies, which express the limits of human knowledge, may be of profound significance.

Just where these different theories and conflicting ideas fit into the overarching panoply of our discussion, remains to be seen in due time. Though a good general understanding of most scientific principles and of the deep complexity involved in the physics of creation would be invaluable here, we can only go so far. In any event, it is not my intent to enter into a scientific or a metaphysical discussion about the merits of the existence of God, but by the end of our journey, we shall see that the questions we ask about pain and suffering will lead us right to the heart of that very issue. Obviously, there is a real dispute about this in the scientific world, and the facts and theories that we have briefly mentioned here must fit somewhere into the great mosaic that is one truth. We will briefly return to them later in our exploration.

PART VI: GENESIS REVISITED – THE PROBLEM OF PAIN & SUFFERING

Let us return to Genesis and focus on two points: First, the scientific view of creation differs greatly from the view of Genesis. However, despite the great wealth of scientific knowledge, science has no proven explanation for the ultimate cause of creation. It does not know what caused the Big Bang. Second, if God is the force behind the scientific principles responsible for creation, then we still have the same problem we started with. For despite the long odds against our existence, God has coaxed us into being and nurtured us along. As a result, we find ourselves nestled into a remote corner of an obscure galaxy: One of hundreds of billions of other galaxies within a vast universe of astounding power, order, and beauty.

In the face of all of this effort, culminating in the development of conscious life of beings made in His own divine image, He then declines to interact with us, at least overtly. *If He is out there, how do we know?*

The point and purpose of this book is not to attempt to prove the existence of God, but to seek Him out where He is. From this point forward, this book explicitly assumes the existence of God. We cannot point to Him and say, "There He is!" Nor can we offer any sensory evidence that He exists. Ultimately, His presence or existence must be inferred or felt or believed as dictated by the facts and circumstances of our individual lives. We will not concern ourselves with that here. He exists.

Fine, but where is He? If He is God, He must be everywhere and must be aware of everything, for omnipresence and omniscience are part of the very definition of God. However, when we need Him most, when we feel that only He can help us, we cannot find Him. It is one thing to assume the existence of God, but it is an entirely different matter to explain why, if He exists, He is not more responsive to our most urgent needs and dire pleas. If our God exists, He must exist somewhere and it is the task of this book to look for Him in the darkest caves, where His light is most needed and most lacking.

Specifically, we will explore and answer the question of the ages: Why does the God of love and mercy permit the suffering of the innocents?

This is a bigger question then you can possibly imagine. From the outset, it is important to remember that the issue of pain and suffering is itself a creation problem. In fact, it is **the** creation problem. Its scope, therefore, is as big and as deep and as complex as creation itself. Accordingly, its explanation has vast ramifications, as we shall see. It is our task to explain the cause of pain and suffering in the context of a loving Creator.

In the end, ironically, we shall be able to say that God allows pain and suffering because He loves us. Though this is true, it explains nothing. It is the short answer, but it sheds no light on the subject. The complete explanation, though simple in some respects, encompasses everything. In many ways, it is not unlike the great quest of science to uncover the Theory of Everything.

We, also, embark upon a similar quest. It has a vast dimension, which extends to every corner of the universe. As we try to solve the problem of pain and suffering, we shall see that it, too, will lead us to the mind of God at the heart of creation. It is our holy grail, the holy grail of the spiritual community. It will astonish many to learn that the pursuit of these two quests, both scientific and spiritual, will lead us to the same place: The holy grail is indeed one truth.

Each of these quests is pure and will enrich us as we pursue them. From either side, these quests will teach us more than we can anticipate, answer questions we have not thought to ask, and fill us with wisdom beyond our expectations. Each quest will teach us who we are destined to be, what we were made to be. Fulfilling these quests will ultimately result in rewards of the highest order and transcend our current understanding of life.

Before we can pursue our quest, we must more precisely define the problem. The problem of pain and suffering is the juxtaposition of an infinitely loving God with His long-suffering creatures.

If there is no God, there is no problem. There is no mystery. Secular science can well explain the cause of hurricanes, lightning strikes, floods, and earthquakes. It is the assumption of and a belief in God that poses the problem. Why would He include these sources of destruction in His universe without protecting us from them? Why won't He answer our most desperate prayers?

I am not here concerned with the inhumanity of one person to another. As members of the human race, we well understand our potential to commit evil acts. Nor am I concerned with the problems posed by nature or life that we have the power to endure and overcome. For in enduring and overcoming, we see that we have the strength necessary to survive. The problem to be addressed here is that of natural disasters and the misfortunes of fate, the sorts of problems that only God has the power to prevent or to ameliorate. The kinds of problems we see ravage our brothers and sisters without an equitable offset of good.

The problem to be addressed is really one of justice. We cannot deny that many suffer. From birth defects to abject poverty, from disease to natural calamity, we are well aware of the great and debilitating obstacles confronting men, women, and children throughout the world. In large part, they who suffer are innocent. Their sins did not cause their suffering. Life is not fair. They have done no more, and no less, than any of us to deserve their fate.

I do not argue that they are not sinners, but that we all are sinners. I do not argue that we don't deserve some of the suffering that besets us, for, in a spiritual sense, we all do. Rather, the question becomes one of justice: Can we say that there is justice in the world when we consider the way in which this suffering is distributed? It defies reason to say so. Our own experiences clearly discredit this theory. Some suffer terribly throughout their lives, and others live lives of unearned luxury and privilege. Even Jesus, when asked, denied that this kind of suffering was deserved, the prevalent thinking of the time,

> "Do you think that these Galileans were the greatest sinners in Galilee just because they suffered this? By no means! But I tell you, you will all come to the same end unless you reform. Or take those eighteen who were killed by a falling tower in Siloam. Do you think they were more guilty than anyone else who lived in Jerusalem? Certainly not!" Luke 13:2-5

The concept of justice is at the heart of the problem. One of the reasons I was attracted to the question of pain and suffering was that I never thought I heard a satisfactory explanation. As in the reading of a good mystery, the more dead ends one uncovers, the more curious one becomes. The harder and longer I searched, the more determined I became to find a solution.

It is an intractable problem. Very few have a good grasp of it. Of all of the people I ever heard discuss it, and of all the authors I have read who wrote about it, one who has come close is C. S. Lewis. Lewis was a well-known 20th century British author and Oxford professor. Though once an atheist, he became widely recognized as a Christian thinker. In his book, The Problem of Pain, he discusses the elements of pain and suffering, and offers many thought-provoking arguments. Though Lewis has a profound sense of the issues involved, I do not believe he has adequately addressed the demands of justice, which are so fundamental to the resolution of this issue. At one point he complains that we tend to exaggerate the problem of pain. He argues that an individual can only suffer so much and that there can be no more pain after that:

> *"We must never make the problem of pain worse than it is by vague talk about the 'unimaginable sum of human misery'... There is no such thing as a sum of suffering, for no one suffers it. When we have reached the maximum that a single person can suffer, we have, no doubt, reached something horrible, but we have reached all the suffering there ever can be in the universe. The addition of a million fellow-sufferers adds no more pain."*[26]

Lewis may have a point, especially from the perspective of one individual, but what does it say about God? Is God incapable of feeling or recognizing the "unimaginable sum of human misery?" If we deserve our own pain, if it helps us to repent and return to God, and if it is justly measured to our sins, it is acceptable and righteous. However, how are we to encounter the God of love amidst all of the senseless pain and suffering we see in the world? How do we call Him merciful and just? What kind of God do we believe in if He allows the enormity of the suffering that occurs? It is not just about one man's tolerance for pain, but about the God with whom we hope we can relate, let alone worship. This becomes the central issue.

Nevertheless, Lewis has much to offer on this problem and has a great sense of it. He accurately conceives the issue as one of relationship, priority, and purpose – relationship to God; the priority of that relationship above all else; and the use of pain and suffering as a tool to call us back to Him. He senses that the answers revolve around love and necessity. He sees that the answer will require not only understanding, but dialogue, a response. In all that he senses and describes, he is on the right track, but he does not fully comprehend it, as he readily admits. There is a greater need for justice than he implies and a deeper level of purpose.

It is noticeably clear, however, that Lewis sees this as a creation problem in some sense, that it lurks in the shadows of creation and is intrinsic thereto,

> "...try to exclude the possibility of suffering which the order of nature and the existence of free wills involve, and you find that you have excluded life itself...Perhaps this isn't the 'best of all possible' universes, but the only possible one."[27]

C. S. Lewis, therefore, puts his finger on the essential point: *"Perhaps we do not realize the problem of enabling finite free wills to exist with Omnipotence."*[28] Already the focus has changed, and the perspective has shifted. To properly address the problem of pain and suffering, we cannot look at it from our own perspective, but from His. What is God's purpose in creation, and how does He achieve it?

If only I were God, I would create the world far differently (At least, that is what we all would say). Perhaps, it would be along the utopian lines of John Lennon's *Imagine*. Perhaps, it would be even more idyllic. We each have an imagination that can depict various and wondrous idealized settings, but do we have the imagination to create what God created?

Do we have the imagination to pronounce that the divergent declarations of Einstein, Sagan, Leibniz, and Hawking all proclaim the truth? For maybe "God does play dice with the universe," and maybe there is "nothing for a Creator to do," and maybe this is the 'best of all possible universes,' and maybe we can "know the mind of God." When the question of pain and suffering is addressed from His perspective, it will distinctly reshape the perception of reality and justice that we have and hold.

Genesis was never meant to be scientific truth. It addresses completely different issues. Once upon a time, it may have been mistaken for an explanation of the physical creation of the universe, but this was a period of time that predated science, a time when science was ill considered and undeveloped. Few viable alternative theories existed. Our view of the physical world was ill informed and wrong. But a fair and even cursory reading of the Bible plainly reveals that the Bible has almost nothing to say about any of the physical sciences. Outside of a few passing references to astrology at the birth of Christ, or to engineering in the building of the Ark of the Covenant, there are precious few discussions of any of the hard sciences. One would be hard pressed to find serious allusions to geometry, medicine, biology, mathematics, engineering, chemistry, geology, physics, or any other scientific endeavors. It is not the purpose of the Bible to speak to these issues. It is not the purpose of Genesis to give a scientific account of creation. Genesis is simply a story meant to engage us, and for thousands of years, it has. It possesses truth and great meaning, but not scientific truth. Its aim is much higher.

The God of Genesis does not lie, but He does employ imagery to make a point and to speak to us on our own level, and in our own language. To put it another way, the Bible does not always speak the literal truth, to do so would be to condemn us all. It does not speak to us through mathematical equations, though some in science and mathematics are convinced that it must be God's true language. God speaks to us in ways we can all understand and in ways that we find engaging, as does the creation story in the Bible, as does science in everyday life.

Genesis has obviously been highly effective in this regard. We still debate it. We still ardently discuss its meaning. Though a myth in form, it has profound implications. Even the very idea that God speaks to us at all is astonishing. Though the creation story may not consist entirely of literal truth, it is still relevant to the creation story of science. To the extent that science is true, and to the extent that science uncovers new truth, Genesis must accept and incorporate it. Genesis is compatible to all truth. It accepts the truth of science, but does not pursue it, guide it, or explain it. The only scientific premise it advances is that God created the universe. As to the question of how the physical universe was created, Genesis has nothing further to say.

Similarly, science has little to say about God. The premise that God created the universe is not strictly scientific. It is outside the realm of science. It is metaphysical and not a question of physical reality. Most any scientist will acknowledge this. The 'theory of God' cannot be tested or proven. Science examines, tests, and explores physical law and properties, but God exists outside of the physical arena. As Genesis does not speak to scientific truth, science cannot directly speak to God. It has no tools, no facility, and therefore, no ability to speak authoritatively about God.

Yet, the study of science should be open to the possibility of the existence of God. It need not pursue it, but it should recognize that not all truth is physical. If science comes to recognize the physical reality that there are practical limits to knowledge, then is it not possible that these limits are significant and meaningful?

It is at this very point that science and spirituality converge. When, and if, science uncovers the Theory of Everything, only the metaphysical issues will remain. Hawking is right: We will then confront the mind of God with full knowledge and from every possible perspective. Science will rejoin the spiritual quest and renew the exploration of the meaning of human life, the one question that will remain.

For us and for our journey, the role of science is simply the pursuit of truth: The development of tools to see God more clearly. Science will help us find God where He is. Proven science and true faith, both lead to God. They are in harmony, even if our understanding falls short.

PART VII: RETURN TO THE GARDEN OF EDEN

What, then, does Genesis really tell us about God's creation? What is the significance of the Tree of Knowledge of Good and Bad? What is the relationship between creation and pain and suffering? We are now in position to begin to address the key questions of Genesis, as they relate to our spiritual quest. Our journey ultimately seeks to explain the cause of pain and suffering allowed by God. Genesis conjoins the creation story with the issue of pain and suffering. They are presented side by side from the very beginning. In chapter one of Genesis, we are created, and in chapter three, we are banished from Eden and left to suffer the consequences of fate. Genesis makes this connection, but it is up to us to explore it. The remainder of this book will do so, part by part. For the remainder of this chapter, we will address the primary meaning and direction of Genesis.

When we seek meaning out of Genesis, we must first realize Genesis is as much in the business of presenting questions as it is delivering answers. Even so, good questions are the foundation of all wisdom, and Genesis has great questions.

The Book of Genesis is basically divided into two parts: First, there is, of course, the creation story. Whether myth or fact, it is little more than an assertion of God's will to create the universe. In the exercise of His will, we come easily to recognize the awesome power of God. The incomprehensible act of creation has captivated the minds of all humanity from the beginning of time. As science attempts to plumb the depths of this enigma, it is all the more fascinating. We are more than ever bedazzled by its indescribable beauty, incalculable power, and mysterious origins. Mathematically, artistically, scientifically, and philosophically it is utterly marvelous. If this is to be the power of God that shines forth, then we stand in perpetual awe of His handiwork.

The balance of Genesis is primarily a story of nation building, of relationship. It is the search for and the creation of a people who agree to trust and obey the will of God in exchange for the promised-land and innumerable descendants. Thus, God interacts with Noah, Abraham, Isaac, Jacob, and Joseph to further the development of such a people and such a covenant.

The very basic premise of Genesis is, therefore, that God is an immensely powerful Creator, and we must obey Him to secure His protection, peace, and prosperity. It is my impression that this has been the primary historical approach to the understanding of Genesis.

With Abraham, obedience transcends to faith, but the rock of Genesis has always been the concept of obedience. It defines our primary relationship and duty to God. It is easy to say this is a fair reading of the Book of Genesis. The banishment of Adam and Eve from Eden and the Doctrine of the Fall of Man are predicated upon the single act of disobedience, symbolized by the biting of the forbidden apple. It is clear that Adam was not to eat the fruit of the Tree of Knowledge and clear that he disobeyed this rule. The consequences of this intransigence were severe. It is, therefore, easy to conclude that Genesis is asserting the primacy of obedience to God in all things.

But it is not. The creation story of Genesis is more myth than fact, a moral, a metaphor. It is not primarily about obedience, though there is most certainly that. Obedience is a good introduction. It is low hanging fruit, but it is not the heart of the matter. God is the Creator, but that is not enough either. We must obey, but why? Is it simply because God is powerful, and we must fear Him, or is there more to the story? Genesis is not primarily about obedience, though obedience is important, first and last, as we shall see. Genesis is primarily about destiny, about discovering whom we are.

Genesis seeks to confront us with two questions: Why did God create us, and how did God create us? In order to understand our God, and our relationship to Him and His creation, we must try to understand these two things. In other words, we must try to determine why God decided to create us and what method He used to create us. From there, we must ask, *what is our purpose*? The answers to these questions will define who we are.

These questions and the clues to their solution are what are at the core of Genesis. It is these that are of primary importance under the surface of the Genesis metaphor. The answers to these questions will also ultimately help us to solve the problem of pain and suffering and to thus uncover the logic and justice inherent in the divine act of creation. Indeed, it will renew our faith, for a God without logic or justice is imperfect and illusory.

One of the most beautiful aspects of God and His creation, and truth in general, is that it is often so simple. As a boy, I often marveled over the power inherent in a simple rainfall. The confluence of events that result in a billion gentle raindrops that can nurture the land and form the creeks, the rivers, and the oceans: The power and potential of small things in great numbers. Likewise, the answers to the questions emanating from Genesis can be fascinatingly simple. Like the raindrops, however, they may flow through the hills and valleys of other questions and ideas before settling in the powerful ocean of truth.

Let us look at the first question of Genesis: Why did God create us? Though there may be a simple answer to this question, Genesis does not provide it. The second part of Genesis, the part that describes the formation of God's people, seems to suggest that we were created in order to have a relationship with God. This is neatly summarized early in the Book of Exodus when God speaks to Moses: "I will take you as my own people, and I will be your God." Ex. 6:7. However, there is no indication as to why God would want to bother with us as His people. Why does God choose to have people?Genesis raises this question but provides no clear answer. Later, we will return to focus on this issue exclusively in Chapter 5.

For now, let us consider the one clue that is given to us by Genesis. Though we are not yet clear on God's desire for our creation, we are emphatically told one thing about His creation: *"It is good."* Genesis 1:31[22]

Though we have stated the story of Adam and Eve is a myth or a moral making a larger point, it is not quite possible to deflect the plain and literal meaning of this bold statement. *"It is good."* There is no need to look for deeper or hidden meaning here. It is either good or it isn't.

In many ways, it is really the quintessential question of this book. *Is the creation of God's universe good?* The fact we ask the question does not bode well for the answer. If it is so obviously good, then why does this question even arise? If it is good, it doesn't always seem to be. In order for us to successfully complete our quest, we will have to arrive at the same conclusion – that it is good. Though we must concede that this is a daunting task, it is an extraordinary opportunity for understanding.

And so, we are back to the idea of justice. If it is good, it must be fair and just – not just for some, but for all. Does the goal of creation justify the means? If the goal is to create life, does our universe represent the best way to do it? Is there any other way conscious life could have been created or does God have no real choice in the essential means of creation?

These are the questions as we go forward. If we are successful in our quest, we will have discovered that God's creation is good. We will have discovered that His creation stems from His love and is an incomparable gift. We will have discovered the goal of creation, to create life, is a worthy goal and the means of creation are justified.

If we are allowed, for a moment, to presume that this holy grail can be found, then we can allow ourselves to speculate on what it means when God says that *"It is good."* For when God says it, it must be good indeed.

From this succinct proclamation, we can infer several things: Chief among them is love must be involved. From all we know and sense about God, from the way that we define Him and from the way that we desire Him to be, love is always involved. If God is the Absolute Energy that created the universe, then it is from that act that we recognize His power. If He decided to create us *"in His own image,"* in order that we may be His people, then it is from that decision that we recognize His love.

If we define God as all that is good in the highest possible order, then we recognize that when He says, *"it is good,"* His creation must be of the highest possible order. For when He says, *"it is good,"* then it is good in the eyes of God. It is good in the way that God is good. From this, I believe we can rightly infer that if "it is good," it is not only well designed and well made, but well intended. It is motivated by the infinite love of a loving God.

In the beginning of this chapter, we saw the God of Genesis as a creator, giver, provider, and loving friend. If creation is good, and if God is the God we wish Him to be (i.e., loving, merciful, powerful, just, wise, and perfect), then we have every right to expect a creation built on those attributes. If the source of creation is love and perfection, then we have the right to expect the result of creation to be a manifestation of love and perfection.

Therefore, the question becomes, *can we call our universe a manifestation of love and perfection?* At first blush, this is hard to know. We are tempted many times over to say no. But there is enough good and love in this world to temper our initial reaction and draw us into deeper contemplation. If our God is a God of love –Creator, Giver, Provider, and Friend – then love must be an integral part of our understanding of creation and of creation's relationship to pain and suffering. It is a concept that we can well appreciate.

As St. Paul tells us, love is a dynamic force: *"the greatest of these is love."* It is the one force that we know that could conceivably create the type of universe that we long for. It is a force we are well equipped to explore and understand. We have all experienced this force of love. We are all affected and motivated by it. We value it greatly. We seek it desperately. We know that its removal is a source of pain and frustration strong enough to warp and distort normal development. When available in just proportion, its influence is positive and dynamic, both individually and communally. Love is the undercurrent of our being and is integral to our most cherished relationships. Our most cherished creations come from love and all true art, in every form, stems from it. Ideally, we, ourselves, are born from love and desire to procreate through love. It is a force found deep inside of us, which seeks its way out, compelling us toward some other person or goal. It would come as no surprise to any of us that love may be the force for good that was the impetus for creation.

In God, we would expect love to be an even higher force. In God, it would be perfected. Such a love would naturally be expected to be creative and outward looking. The product of a perfect love, God's creation, should likewise be perfect and everlasting. The force of love from God, unleashed on His creation, would continue to create from the beginning and onward for all time. Like an unending chain reaction, a perfect love would ignite a flame that never stops growing, giving, and reaching out.

From the beginning, Genesis asks us to ponder the reasons and circumstances of our being. At the very least, we have begun to meet this challenge. Through our knowledge of God, through the Word of God, and through our own intuition, we surmise that love is at the core of creation. It is a mystery to which we will return.

The second question of Genesis is: How did God create us? In examining this second question, we should first note it is not a question of scientific cause and effect. We will leave that question to the scientists. In this question, we explore His method: What are the circumstances of our existence?

In raising this question, Genesis is a bit more on point. The answer is directly given, though we are left to determine what it means. Genesis asserts that God created us *"in His own image."*[30] To be created in the image of God is quite a concept. What are we to make of it?

If God is a God of perfect love, and if He created us in His own image out of perfect love with all of the power and wisdom at His disposal, then we must expect His creation to be perfect. Yet, we are not perfect. How can this be? How, then, are we created in His own image?

In order to understand God, we must recognize that even God has logical limits. As children, we pondered cumbersome and childish conundrums. Can God create a rock so big that He cannot lift it? The answer to that, of course, is that He cannot. It is a logical impossibility. If He created us perfectly, we would rival even Him. That again, is a logical impossibility. There can only be one omnipotent God. We must necessarily be created with limits. Any limit, however, is an imperfection. Therefore, it is impossible that we could be perfect.

The real question is whether His creation, taken as a whole, is perfect within the context of necessary logical limits. He created us *"in His own image."* We must determine what this means.

As we have already seen, we know it cannot mean that we can rival God in power, wisdom, or other physical attributes; for if He is to remain a God, He must have dominion over us. But there is one essential aspect of humanity more important than all the rest. It can be fully endowed in us, without being diminished in Him. This attribute is, of course, free will. As God is free to act of His own will, in His sphere, so are we, in ours. We are indeed, therefore, created in His image in the most essential way of all.

So, therefore, to answer the questions as to why we are created and how we are created, we must, on first impression, say that we are created out of love - with free will and limited power. Logically speaking, this is a creation to the fullest extent possible within necessary limits. The creation, therefore, appears to be a perfect product of perfect love even though we, ourselves, are imperfect.

Conceptually and theoretically, it is impossible to imagine a greater God or a greater gift from a loving Creator: Created from love and given free will to the fullest extent possible.

Why, then, does He abandon us?

Chapter Two
MY GOD, MY GOD,
WHY HAVE YOU FORSAKEN ME?

*Nothing exists; all is a dream. God - man – the world, -the sun,
the moon, the wilderness of stars: a dream, all a dream, they
have no existence. Nothing exists, save empty space—and you!*

...

*Strange! That you should not have suspected, years ago,
centuries, ages, aeons ago! For you have existed, companionless,
through all the eternities. Strange, indeed, that you should not
have suspected that your universe and its contents were only
dreams, visions, fictions! Strange, because they are so frankly
and hysterically insane—like all dreams: a God who could
make good children as easily as bad, yet preferred to make bad
ones; who could have made every one of them happy, yet never
made a single happy one; who made them prize their bitter life,
yet stingily cut it short; who gave his angels eternal happiness
unearned, yet required his other children to earn it; who gave
his angels painless lives, yet cursed his other children with biting
miseries and maladies of mind and body; who mouths justice,
and invented hell---mouths mercy, and invented hell---mouths
Golden Rules, and forgiveness multiplied seventy times seven,
and invented hell; who mouths morals to other people, and has
none himself; who frowns upon crimes, yet commits them all;
who created man without invitation, then tries to shuffle the
responsibility for man's acts upon man, instead of honorably
placing it where it belongs, upon himself; and finally, with
altogether divine obtuseness, invites this poor abused slave to
worship him!*
No. 44, The Mysterious Stranger[1]
Mark Twain

It is not useful to debate that this is a cruel, brutally harsh, and
unforgiving world. We know it is. It haunts us daily. It drives some of

us into depression and despair. Mark Twain, the famous and wildly popular humorist, penned bitter thoughts at the end of his life in his last novel, published posthumously. Though there is some scholarly debate, it appears that he meant them.

The human race remains remarkably optimistic and resilient in the face of endless tragedy. There is, however, no denying that we have suffered horribly. Some of this suffering is our own fault, caused by our own hands and our own choices. However, much of it is not.

At times we seem no better situated than Prometheus, tied to a rock at the top of a mountain, buffeted by every element, beset by a vulture, fighting to stay alive. How long can we last? Even those who avoid tragedy are slowly eviscerated over the long journey of life, until nothing remains. As Twain himself might put it, we are "a museum of diseases, a home of impurities," which "begins as dirt and departs as stench."[2]

Though I do not wish to be as cynical as Twain, we must clearly see our dilemma. Mankind suffers. It suffers greatly. This is a fact upon which we usually do not wish to brood. The human race has a remarkable ability to repress what it finds abhorrent or to, at least, distance it from our daily consciousness. We block out the painful memories so we can move forward and focus on the present. This quality is a great blessing and a helpful, if not courageous, trait.

But our reality and our true circumstance must be examined for what it is, clinically, if we can. If the God of love created us, He has left us vulnerable, and we bleed.

It is of no use to say that good sometimes comes from evil. It is of no use to say that this is part of God's plan. For how can it be? Why would He? Where is the logic in this plan? Where is the justice?

We have been looking to make sense of this for so long. Are we so blind that we cannot see it? Is our God simply an imperfect invention of ours that falters at this breaking point? Are we stuck with the musings of Mark Twain who wonders about "the utter inconsequence of humanity in the divine perspective."[3] If we cannot discern God in this plan, then none exists. We have faith even in pursuing the problem, but the problem requires an answer.

Here we explore the magnitude of the problem. It is a grueling task. We have become hardened by constant exposure to horror. We have retreated further and further into ourselves in the face of an endless cycle of tragic news broadcast daily. Masters of repression and justification, as we are subjects of oppression, we nimbly justify the inconceivable and stoically carry on. We must stop running. We must open ourselves up, once again, and look innocently at the horrific conflagration of past historical events. We must feel the suffering afresh and relive the pain if we are to deeply consider who we are and why we exist.

The following events represent a far from comprehensive list of some of the most well-known and tragic natural disasters to have occurred in human history. There are many, many others, too numerous to list, but they all have in common one compelling idea: None of them were caused by the acts or ill will of any man or woman. None of them could have been stopped by anyone, but God.

I.   In 1918, 21 million people worldwide suffered and died from the Spanish influenza.

II. On July 28, 1976, a major earthquake occurred in Tangshan China. 250,000 died. Another 164,000 were severely injured.

III. On May 8, 1902, life on the island of Martinique was obliterated by the eruption of Mount Pelee. 30,000 people perished within seconds of the explosion. There were only 2 survivors.

IV. In 1883, on the island of Krakatau in Indonesia, a volcano erupts leaving over 36,000 dead. The force of the explosion was so great that it could be heard in Australia – over two thousand miles away.

While the two men walked on farther toward Sodom the Lord remained standing before Abraham.

Then Abraham drew nearer to Him and said: "Will you sweep away the innocent with the guilty? Suppose there were fifty innocent people in the city; would You wipe out the place, rather than spare it for the sake of the fifty innocent people within it? Far be it from you to do such a thing, to make the innocent die with the guilty, so that the innocent and the guilty would be treated alike! Should not the judge of all the world act with justice?"

The Lord replied, "If I find fifty innocent people in the city of Sodom, I will spare the whole place for their sake."

Genesis 18:22-26

XI.   *In 1346, the Black Plague strikes Europe and Asia. One third of the entire population is dead within 6 years.*

XII. *On All Saints Day, 1755, in Lisbon, Portugal, an earthquake causes immense devastation to a thriving city. What the earthquake doesn't destroy, fire and a resultant tsunami does. 60,000 are left dead. So fractured is the faith and psyche of the citizens, that the Jesuits are forced to leave the city.*

XIII. *In Kobe, Japan, an earthquake strikes on January 17, 1995. The quake registers 7.2 on the Richter scale. Fires are rampant. 6,300 die and another 43,000 are injured. Over 180,000 buildings are left in ruins. It is estimated that it will take 10 years to rebuild the city.*

XIV. *In Bangladesh, a cyclone devastates the country in 1970. 500,000 victims are claimed.*

XV.   *On September 8, 1900, a hurricane devastates Galveston, Texas. Over 2,600 homes are destroyed leaving over 10,000 homeless.*

XVI. *Cyclone Tracy reaches land early Christmas morning in 1974 in Darwin, Australia. 75 are killed and 40,000 more left homeless. Ninety percent of the town is completely destroyed.*

XVII. The potato famine strikes Ireland in the 1840s. It is due to an uncontrollable fungal infection. Over one and a half million Irish perish. Another 1.6 million flee the country, thereby reducing the overall population of the country by one-third.

XVIII. In 1992, Gomec, Turkey, suffers through an avalanche which kills 125 people, half of the total population of the village. Several hundred more perish in nearby villages.

XIX. Torrential rains lead to a flash flood on the Big Thompson River in Colorado. 139 are killed on January 31, 1976.

XX. In the period from 1981 – 1985, Ethiopia loses 20,000 of her children per month due to famine.

Abraham spoke up again: "See how I am presuming to speak to my Lord, though I am but dust and ashes! What if there are five less than fifty innocent people? Will you destroy the city because of those five?"
"I will not destroy it," he answered, "if I find forty-five there." But, Abraham persisted, saying, "What if only forty are found there?" He replied, "I will forbear doing it for the sake of the forty."
Genesis 18:27-29.

XXI. The discovery of America by Christopher Columbus brings European diseases to the new land. Over the next 400 years, it is estimated that 90 million native-Americans perish due to these diseases. By 1900, the native-American population had dropped to less than 10 million from what once was 100 million.

XXII. In Tokyo, Japan, 150,000 are left dead, due to an earthquake in 1923.

XXIII. *In the province of Shaanxi, China, in the year 1556, 830,000 Chinese are killed by a disastrous earthquake. Many are buried alive in the caves where they are living.*

XXIV. *On, August 24, 1992, Hurricane Andrew creates$25 billion worth of damage. 80,000 Florida homes are destroyed.*

XXV. *On November 13, 1985, in Nevado Del Ruiz, Columbia, 21,000 villagers out of a total population of 23,000 die in a devastating volcano. A wall of mud and ash 130 feet high came crashing down upon the village.*

XXVI. *In 1993, the Mississippi River overflows in the United States. 70,000 are left homeless. Damage totals exceed $12 billion.*

XXVII. *On April 29, 1991, another cyclone devastates the country of Bangladesh and kills over 140,000 people.*

XXVIII. *The Tri State Tornado devastates 3 mid-western states in 1925. 689 Americans were killed.*

XXIX. *The San Francisco earthquake hits the United States on April 18, 1906, killing 500 people and causing vast economic loss.*

XXX. *From 1826 – 1834, India suffers a Cholera Epidemic. Millions die worldwide.[4]*

Then he said, "Let not my Lord grow impatient if I go on. What if only thirty are found there?" He replied, "I will forebear doing it if I can find but thirty there."

Still he went on, "Since I have thus dared to speak to my Lord, what if there are no more than twenty?"

"I will not destroy it," he answered, "for the sake of the twenty."

But he still persisted: "Please let not my Lord grow angry
if I speak up this last time. What if there are at least ten there?"
"For the sake of those ten," he replied, "I will not destroy it."
Genesis 18:22-32

Tragedy comes in many forms and in many ways. It is an inescapable part of our human condition. It may march slowly and inexorably towards us. It may strike suddenly and without warning. It may linger in our consciousness or be branded upon our hearts. Its pain may involve very many or very few. It is an enormous topic. An exhaustive analysis is not important, though the firm realization of its existence, and perhaps even of its essence, is necessary to our understanding.

It is the primary concern of this book to examine the vast and pervading scope of tragedy allowed by God, against the backdrop of a creation claimed by Him to be good. The types of tragedies just reviewed are the most vexing. They are not in any way caused by the evil acts of any man or woman. As such, they are known as events of non-moral evil. Yet, God has allowed it all, and it is useless to say that enough good has come from such overwhelming loss to justify it.

Is it more useful to consider the tragedy of one or the demise of many in this quest? Perhaps this is an unfair question, but it is difficult to grasp the concept of large-scale calamity. It is nearly impossible to comprehend it with true understanding and empathy. Our emotions cannot truly embrace it. An individual cannot process or digest the enormity of it. It is just too big; such loss cannot be heartfelt in the way that it deserves.

The loss of a child, a spouse, or a parent is one of the most heart wrenching and personally tragic events in any lifetime. It would be difficult to feel more emotional loss. Yet each individual lost is a child, a spouse, or a parent and could be so mourned. If 10,000 deaths occurred simultaneously, however, no one could emotionally process such a loss 10,000 times. We are not capable of it. Any effort to understand the tragedy of this world, must therefore begin with the pain and senseless loss of even one.

Monsey, New York

A three-year-old boy was dragged to death after he got off a school bus and the elastic band attached to his mittens got caught in the door, police said. When the bus took off, Chaim Horovits was dragged about 100 feet, hitting his head on the road Tuesday after the band snapped, police said. The boy's 5-year-old brother ran home to call for help, but Chaim was dead when paramedics arrived. The bus driver was unaware that the boy was being dragged, police said.

CHICAGO TRIBUNE
January 16, 2003

Chicago, Illinois

A ten-year-old boy accidentally strangled himself on a towel dispenser Thursday morning at a South Side coin laundry. Police said Christopher Craig, of the 8000 block of South Wood Street, went into the bathroom of the Park Plaza Coin Laundry, 8304 S. King Drive, placed his head in the loop of a cloth towel hanging from a dispenser and spun around, hanging himself.

CHICAGO TRIBUNE
April 2, 1999

Apple Valley, California

Two sisters who had just witnessed their mother give birth to twins were killed in a fiery collision after their car was rear-ended by a drunken driver, authorities said Sunday. Thomas Romero and three daughters were stopped at a red light when another vehicle failed to stop, driving into the back of Romero's car, the sheriff's department said. The car caught fire, Romero escaped with Jennifer, 16, who was sitting in the front passenger seat, but the fire kept him from rescuing his other two daughters in the back seat—Jessica, 10, and Jackie, 14. They died in the blaze. The family was returning from a hospital, where Romero's wife had just given birth to twins, police said.

LOS ANGELES TIMES
December 22, 1997

Independence, Missouri

A boy who became tangled in a seat belt outside his mother's car when it was stolen died Tuesday after being dragged for miles at speeds up to 80 m.p.h. Motorists flashed lights and honked horns as the car sped down Interstate Highway 70. The boy was dragged for 5 or 6 miles until the driver pulled onto another road as three other vehicles followed behind.

When the suspect stopped at a red light, the three vehicles blocked him in. The man tried to flee but was wrestled to the ground by the motorists.

The unidentified boy, whom, police said was about 6 or 7, had been left in the vehicle, its engine running, while his mother ran into a store. The suspect reportedly was trying to push the boy from the car when the child became tangled.

CHICAGO TRIBUNE
February 23, 2000

Six Mile, Alabama

There is fate. There is tragedy. And then there is love.

Highway 25, a ribbon of leaf-scattered asphalt in rural Alabama, connects them all. It connects two women, steaming toward each other from opposite ends of the county, one looking for the other. On the afternoon of Nov. 17, Sheila Wentworth left her home and headed north on Highway 25.

At the same time, Dorris Jean Hall left her home and headed south on Highway 25.

As the two women approached a bend in the road, both in Jeep Cherokees, they collided head-on at 60 m.p.h.

Firefighters tried to save them, cutting open the cars with blowtorches. But the damage was too great. When the coroner called family members, the shock was multiplied.

Hall, 52, and Wentworth were sisters. They were on their way to each other's houses. Hall's husband, Billy Joe, 54, was driving. He also died.

"What are the odds of this?" Wentworth's husband, Brian,

asked as he took a long, sad drag on his cigarette. "One in a million? One in a billion?"

At the funeral Thursday, the pastor gave a sermon on friendship. And the warmth of family. It is the one sweetener in Six Mile and the surrounding towns. The area, 60 miles south of Birmingham, is short of jobs, long on toil, poor and getting poorer.

People here can tell some horrible car accident stories. Traveling 60 m.p.h. along curvy roads is how they move. But the unbelievable coincidence of this crash—two sisters killed in a head-on collision—is too much for anybody to absorb.

"Sometimes it makes the hair stick up on the back of your neck," said Bo Hall, whose parents were killed.

What put the two sisters on the road that day was their routine. They were doing what they always did, visiting relatives.

That Sunday, Dorris Hall was traveling with her husband and her granddaughter Amber to Centreville. Sheila Wentworth was heading to Montevallo with her nephew Frankie. Neither knew the other was coming. It was an overcast day, but not wet.

Those are the only facts. "After that, we just don't know what happened," said Chuck Martin, the deputy county coroner. "Did they see each other and wave? Did one lose control?"

The children in the cars were both injured, thoughnot critically.
By Jeffrey Gettleman
New York Times News Service
CHICAGO TRIBUNE
November 26, 2002

St. Louis, Missouri

They heard suffering. They couldn't tell what it was or where it came from. But it sounded awful. That was all they knew. Questioned later, they told police only that they heard "something suffering out there."

How horribly right they were.

The noise that residents of an inner-city neighborhood heard just after supper Monday was the sound of a boy being eaten alive by a pack of dogs.

Ten-year-old Rodney McAllister, a chatterbox of a 4th grader, was mauled to death on the concrete basketball court of the park across the street from his family's apartment.

A passerby found Rodney's body the next morning, and now this stunned city wonders why.

Why so many dogs were roaming the park despite repeated calls from neighbors to the animal-control agency. Why adults who heard the howls and moans shut their windows and did nothing. Why Rodney's mother didn't worry when he failed to come home for dinner, or for bedtime, or for school the next morning after heading to the park with his basketball at 5 p.m. on Monday.

St. Louis Police Chief Ron Henderson had few answers Thursday. "In my 30 years on the force, I've never seen anything like this," he said. "I'm not just talking as a chief of police, but as a parent."

Rodney's body was chewed all over. The pathologist suspects the boy was eaten while still alive.

By Stephanie Simon
Los Angeles Times
March 9, 2001

Price County, Wisconsin
In Price County, a 15-year-old boy died when he stood up in a blind to see a deer and was shot in the head by his father.
From an article by Julie Dreardroff
Tribune Staff Reporter
CHICAGO TRIBUNE
December 2001

West Valley City, Utah
A woman looking for her two daughters and three other children drove around in a car without realizing that the girls were locked in the trunk, where they had died of heat stroke.

"This is the horror story inside a horror story," West Valley police Lt. Charles Illsley said. "The mother's in the car,

frantically looking for the children. And they're in the trunk. It's incomprehensible." Temperatures inside the car trunk may have neared 140 degrees, heat so intense that death could come within 30 minutes, the state medical examiner said Monday.

The five children were reported missing after they were playing together Friday afternoon in West Valley, a community west of Salt Lake City, as temperatures approached 96 degrees. They were found about an hour later when police officers and one of the mothers popped the trunk on the 1993 Saturn.

They were identified as sisters Audrey Smith, 2, and Jashea Smith, 6; their cousins, Alisha Richardson, 3, and Ashley Richardson, 6; and a 5-year-old neighborhood friend, McKell Hedden. The children were being watched by Dixie Smith, the mother of Audrey and Jashea. The Richardson girls were her nieces. Detectives had not yet determined how the children got into the car trunk. He said the vehicle has a trunk release latch in the passenger compartment. The trunk is also accessible by pulling down the rear seat.

Associated Press
CHICAGO SUNTIMES
August 1998

Salt Lake City, Utah

A mother and father who made the mistake of taking shelter from a storm under a tree were killed instantly—right before their three youngsters' eyes.

Richard and Lisa Goff died Saturday evening when a thunderstorm with hail, hard rain and a barrage of lightning bolts hit the campground at Crystal Lake, about 60 miles east of Salt Lake City.

The children, 9-year-old Dakota and his sisters Makenzie, 5, and Megan, 18 months, "were basically incoherent" when rescuers arrived, Summit County Sheriff Dave Edmunds said. "They had just seen their parents killed. They were in shock."

The parents, both 34, from the Salt Lake City suburb of West Jordan were sitting on metal chairs when the bolt came down, the woman's sister, Lori Ostler, told a Salt Lake City television station. The location is at the 10,000-foot level in the Uinta Mountains.

The National Oceanic and Atmospheric Administration's tips for safety during lightning storms specifically warn against taking shelter under a tree and tell people to avoid metal objects such as fences or tennis rackets.

For the children, who were hospitalized in good condition, the loss started to sink in Sunday.

"The little girl said several times that she wished her mother was there, but knew she couldn't be," said the family's clerical leader, Bishop Walter Ewell of the Westbrook First Ward of the Church of Jesus Christ of Latter-day Saints. It wasn't clear which girl he was referring to.

"When her grandmother came, she cried and said she knew her mother would never be with her again."

Friends said Megan would cling to her mother and rarely went to anyone else. "It is going to be tough for them," Ewell said.

The children were expected to be released to their grandparents.

"I can deal with one, either of them. I can deal with that. But when both are taken, it's incredible," Ostler said. "How do you begin to keep this family intact? You tell the little boy who saw his parents get killed that they won't be back, they're gone."

Rick Goff worked in an auto body shop and his wife was a homemaker. Friends said the family loved boating, fishing, camping and hiking.

"If it was an outdoorsy thing they did it. They loved riding four-wheelers, snowmobiling," said Eric Hansen, a friend.

With their deaths, 66 people have died in Utah from lightning in the past 52 years, and 130 have been injured. More than half the incidents have happened in July and August.

Associated Press
CHICAGO TRIBUNE
July 22, 2003

Chicago, Illinois

A 2-year-old girl, eluding her mother's attempt to grab her, fell from the third-story bedroom window of a Little Village apartment, her father said Thursday.

Jose Hernandez said his wife was busy setting the alarm clock and he was sitting on his bed talking on the phone to his mother in Mexico at about 10 p.m. Wednesday when his daughter Yalin, ran into the bedroom, jumped up behind him, on the bed and started bouncing. Seconds later, the child plunged out the nearby third-story window as her mother let out a scream and desperately grabbed for Yalin, the 29-year-old father said.

The death was ruled an accident Thursday by the Cook County medical examiner's office.

Jose Hernandez said he dashed outside and found Yalin on the ground. He snatched her up in his arms. "I ask her 'Wake up, wake up,'" he recalled. "She breathed but didn't talk. Yalin was rushed to Mt. Sinai Hospital and transferred to Children's Memorial Hospital where she was pronounced dead.

Fighting back tears during an interview Thursday, Hernandez said his daughter was a playful child who loved soccer. He recalled how she would run into his arms every day after work and yell, "Papi, Papi."

"I ask God why he take my kid," the 29-year-old Hernandez said Thursday. "Why he don't take me? She's too small."

By Angeline Soenarie
Tribune Staff Reporter
CHICAGO TRIBUNE
June 20, 2003

These stories are tortuous to read. In a few moments, the heartbreak of reading them may diminish, but the sadder reality is stories like these happen every day in our world. There are literally hundreds, if not thousands, more stories like them. Many are far worse. One by one they occur. The innocents sometimes die horribly, and we plaintively ask why. My God, my God is this part of your plan? Is this necessary? Can it not be avoided?

If only I were God, this enervating, endless, hopeless tragedy would not be.

Though the preceding stories are immensely painful to consider, they are small tragedies compared to the historical tragedies listed further above. The acute pain and suffering in these individual stories ripple through the friends and families of these victims in untold ways. It lingers there, not easily dissipated, though sometimes somewhat isolated.

The intense pain in these stories, however, may be multiplied exponentially in other circumstances. Past events have led to horrific injury and loss of life. As we have seen before, sometimes it is hundreds that die. Sometimes, whole villages have been lost. At other times, communities have disappeared, and cities have been eradicated. Even whole populations have been destroyed.

Imagine the suffering of the dying, of the injured, of the homeless and the helpless. Imagine the suffering of the orphans and the burdens left on the shoulders of those who survive. Imagine, if you can, the pain in those events. Imagine the sheer hopelessness many must feel. These were not wars or unjustified and preventable acts of man. These were all "Acts of God."

What can be said? It is utterly impossible to comprehend what we have endured and how victimized we are. The stories are real. The catastrophes are well-documented and historical. The grotesque and horrific images of death, starvation, mass graves, and mutilation are not presented here, though they do exist and are part of us, part of our human condition.

Very real, very painful tragedy exists every day, everywhere, and we know with certainty, that more is to come. We must consider why and not be paralyzed in our analysis. We must have clear knowledge yet think with objectivity. Our analysis must not be handicapped by horror or despair. Nor should it fear truth.

The truth is that these horrible tragedies occur continuously. They are avoidable in that the God we commonly believe in has the power to avoid them. But He does not. Could not even one of these have been saved or spared by an infinitely loving God? My God, my God why have you forsaken us?

If only I were God, if only I had the power of God could I even begin to imagine how to allow so much misery and senseless loss to occur in my world and to my children… and do nothing. What are we to make of what Jesus tells us:

> "Consider the ravens; they do not sow, they do not reap, they have neither cellar nor barn—yet God feeds them. How much more important are you than the birds. …Or take the lilies of the field: they do not spin, they do not weave; but I tell you, Solomon in all his splendor was not arrayed like any one of them. If God clothes in such splendor the grass of the field, which grows today and is thrown on the fire tomorrow, how much more will he provide for you."
> Luke 12:24-28.

Can the events and circumstances discussed in this chapter possibly correspond to the good Genesis speaks of in its creation story? Can they possibly be the result of the creation of a loving and merciful God? Or is our loving God simply a fiction, a myth or a coping mechanism? Perhaps, as Twain might say, he is just the best hope of our collective imagination – 'a con man conjured up to fleece us of our sorrows'.

> "You perceive, now, that these things are all impossible, except in a dream. You perceive that they are pure and puerile insanities, the silly creations of an imagination that is not conscious of its freaks –in a word, that they are a dream, and you are the maker of it. The dream-marks are all present - you should have recognized them earlier …
> It is true, that which I have revealed to you: There is no God, no universe, no human race, no earthly life, no heaven, no hell. It is all a Dream, a grotesque and foolish dream. Nothing exists but You. And You are but a Thought—a vagrant Thought, a useless Thought, a homeless Thought, wandering forlorn among the empty eternities!"

He vanished, and left me appalled; for I knew, and realized, that all he had said was true.

No. 44, The Mysterious Stranger[5]

Mark Twain

Chapter Three
PARADISE LOST

Nor only tears
Rained at their eyes, but high winds worse within
Began to rise, high passions – anger, hate
Mistrust, suspicion, discord – and shook sore
Their inward state of mind, calm region once
And full of peace, now lost and turbulent.
Paradise Lost Ch IX: 1121 – 1126
John Milton

It is clear to us now that Paradise has been lost. If it existed once for Adam and Eve, it is altogether gone from our experience. Some say it is promised to us in the future as our ultimate reward, but there is scant evidence of it on Earth. Is it a promise we can trust? How do we know that Paradise ever existed? Are we foolish to believe that it is simply lost and can be rediscovered? How do we know that there is a God who created it?

The evidence of the last chapter demands great skepticism. It is said that logic abhors the random and the chaotic. Indeed, as we saw in Chapter One, Einstein did not care for them much either. They are not the principles that we choose to live by in this world and we are uncomfortable utilizing them as concepts to understand our lives. They are not useful to our security and not helpful to the individual ready to confront the world.

It is ironic, then, that our history, our future and our environment seem to be built on those twin pillars. The story of humanity is a kaleidoscope of social interaction and natural phenomena. As individuals, we can neither control this story, nor understand it. The best we can do is hope to shape it and more often, merely survive it. For a time, we may even flourish within it. This world is chaotic, and we have spent all of written history trying to organize it, civilize it and make sense of our destiny. Our efforts take place in an environment awesomely powerful and complex and wonderfully beautiful all at once.

We have an innate sense of Paradise for these very reasons. We cannot know that Paradise ever existed, but we do know that we are not in it now. We also know that we desire it. We hope for it, and we aspire to it. Verification of Paradise would bring logic to chaos, symmetry to disorder, and peace to our fears. It would bring a sense of divine justice to so much of the pain and suffering we see in this world.

In endeavoring to make sense of our experiences, we have, over the ages, deeply assessed our lives, our consciousness, and our condition. We have been on this journey from the beginning of time. This world of ours makes no sense the way it is. We have never been willing to accept it the way it is. Despite spiritual and intellectual limitations, we strive, seek, and even sense a better place. We sense it even though we have no actual experience of it.

G. K. Chesterton, another brilliant 20th Century Christian thinker and author from Great Britain, spoke very powerfully as to our relationship to this world. In a book called Orthodoxy, he attempts to explain how he came to find his faith after wandering in the desert of the thoughts and theories of his age.

"I felt in my bones; first, that this world does not explain itself. It may be a miracle with a supernatural explanation; it may be a conjuring trick with a natural explanation. But the explanation of the conjuring trick, if it is to satisfy me, will have to be better than the natural explanations I have heard. The thing is magic true or false. Second, I came to feel as if magic must have a meaning, and meaning must have someone to mean it."[1]

Chesterton goes on to conclude that these thoughts and others helped him to see that the 'optimistic' theories of his time, *"had been false and disheartening for this reason, that it had always been trying to prove that we fit in the world. The Christian optimism is based on the fact that we do 'not' fit in to the world. ...The modern philosopher had told me again and again that I was in the right place, and I had still felt depressed even in acquiescence. But I had heard that I was in the wrong place, and my soul sang for joy, like a bird in spring.*"[2]

Thus, on very deep, spiritual levels we have always had a sense that we do not belong here, that there is something more to this life than this world in which we live. There is a sense that our ultimate satisfaction and happiness cannot come from this world. If God exists, there must be something more than this world seems to offer.

Paradise, therefore, may be the last best hope for our God. If we can rediscover or regain Paradise, we will find God, and perhaps an explanation of this difficult world. The premise of this book is that God does exist. If He does exist, then it is fair to expect that He does exist in a place like Paradise. If He does exist, then we can insist that He is bound by logic, justice, and fairness; that He would not be nonsensical; and that, therefore, pain and suffering can be explained and our anguish understood. The existence of Paradise would go a long way toward fulfilling our need for justice and fairness in light of the problems we encountered in the preceding chapter.

An important aspect of the concept of Paradise Lost is the necessary realization that it must have existed if it is now lost. Of course, this is mere conjecture. We cannot know of it. But we do have hope for it. We do imagine it. We do sense it. These are real sentiments. They suggest the possibility of its existence (We have learned to admire the animal kingdom for the instincts and keen senses they possess. Should we so easily disregard our own?).

The concept of Paradise calls to us. It has called to all people, all religions, and all ages. For some, it is hope inspired by fear and anxiety. For others, it is hope inspired by faith and love. Its existence would represent our roots, our home, and our calling. It would dramatically change the perspective of our life here on Earth.

We feel our destiny, but we live in a physical world of hellish indifference. Random actions of natural destruction and disorder beset us and afflict us with fear, insecurity and malaise. It is a never-ending assault, which wages a war of attrition on our hopes, desires, and souls.

As Francis Collins, geneticist, leader of the human genome project, and author, laments, *"must we accept the Dawkins perspective:*

'the universe we observe has precisely the properties we should expect if there is, at bottom, no design, no purpose, no evil and no good, nothing but blind pitiless indifference?'"3

With such darkness surrounding us, how can we know that Paradise exists? What indications do we have? Jesus, of course, refers to it and teaches us of the Kingdom of Heaven. He also promises that a thief next to him on the cross would be with him in Paradise. Other mystics have had visions of it. So, there is some evidence of Paradise, by a few witnesses who have claimed to experience it. Demonstrable proof is otherwise difficult to find.

Genesis, however, in its simple, metaphorical way gives us some extraordinary clues. Adam and Eve are given free rein in Paradise. They may even eat from the fruit of the Tree of Life. The only limitation is that they may not eat from the fruit of the Tree of Knowledge of Good and Evil. They are forbidden only this one thing. Knowledge of good and evil is put off limits.

God grants to Adam and Eve everything else – even eternal life. Eternal life is freely and cheaply provided in Paradise. It is ironic that the humanity, which so fears mortality and so trembles before the existential fear of nothingness, was so freely given the gift of eternal life in Genesis. Modern man so greatly desires the comfort of this gift, or at least the knowledge and hope that it might exist. In the end, with Paradise lost, our fear of nothingness remains. Our only recourse is to faith. A faith to which mankind doggedly clings as it peers into the abyss.

Humanity has always greatly desired this gift of perpetual being. The poets call this desire the immortal longing. Yet, God gave it to humanity, to Adam and Eve, so freely, as if it were nothing, a trifle. Adam and Eve were to live in blissful ignorance, in peace and harmony, in the presence of God for all eternity. Yet, the inescapable inference is that their lives were devoid of significance and understanding. Perhaps, eternal life is not the key to being made in the image and likeness of God.

Prior to eating from the fruit of the Tree of Knowledge, it is written that Adam and Eve were made in the image of God. In Chapter One, we determined this to mean that Adam and Eve had been given the gift of free will. In Paradise, it is apparent that this gift was a limited one. The only command of God in Paradise was not to eat the forbidden fruit. Adam and Eve were not to decide for themselves what was morally right and wrong. The only consequential choice before them was whether to eat from the fruit of this one tree. Though joy was unbounded in Paradise, the gift of free will was indeed constricted.

God seems to value the consequence of this knowledge even more than eternal life. Ironically, it is we who place the greater value on eternal life. Why the disconnect? Why does God place a greater value on the fruit of the Tree of Knowledge of Good and Evil? Is it that eternal life is not the seminal point of our compatibility with God? Is it that the intrinsic power inherent in the fruit of knowledge of good and evil, the power to exponentially broaden the sphere of choice, the power to encroach upon the definition of good, set by God alone in His goodness, is a great danger to us?

Or is the preeminence of the tree of knowledge of good and evil simply a metaphor for the essential requirement of obedience to God in all things? Many believe that this obedience is the essential point of Genesis. They believe that man must serve and obey God as an essential element of righteousness, a right relationship with God. It would follow that with this right relationship with God, eternal life would be of no consequence to us; that God would take care of us.

Though this concept of obedience espouses important truth, it is not the primary truth to be discovered in the story of Adam and Eve. The early Genesis stories are not solely intended to teach us about our relationship to God. They are designed to teach us about ourselves. We have long failed to understand this. The primary point and moral of the story of Adam and Eve is to tell us who we are and what we are. It tells us where we came from and to what we are called. The latter chapters of Genesis simply help us to begin to understand how to get there.

Quite simply, we are beings who cannot live in Paradise. Paradise is a state of being in which we are in total acceptance of the will of God. In such a state, everything is given us. So, it was for Adam and Eve. But Adam and Eve had an essential problem. They lacked understanding.

They were completely innocent, completely unaware. They had little self-knowledge and little awareness of their own significance. The concept of blissful ignorance describes their condition and is key to the understanding of the central teachings of Genesis. Adam and Eve experienced true bliss in the presence of God, but they were ignorant of their circumstances. In this sense, they were not fully actualized, in some ways not greater than the beasts they had dominion over. They were not fully able to understand, and therefore not fully able to realize, themselves, or participate in their world, or relate to their God.

Humanity was designed to be more than the Adam and Eve of Paradise. The biting of the apple simply depicts mankind's innate awareness of good and evil, of right and wrong. This understanding is intrinsic to the definition of humanity. It is the essence of choice and free will.

Once we are aware of good and evil, we become active participants in moral choice. We are free, but imperiled. And if it was ever "forbidden" once, it was for the good of preventing our fall.

In other words, we were created with the knowledge of good and evil and understood our awareness of it. Every subsequent action has required a choice. With each choice, we individually take the steps necessary to define ourselves and to become who we are as individuals. This is the gift of meaningful life, and this is the greatest gift God gives us. It is the ability to become not only who we are, but anything we wish to be.

It is exactly this aspect of our own character, the capacity to understand and to act, which links us to God as beings made in His own image.

God has unlimited power and unlimited choice. We have been granted limited power and unlimited choice to the extent of those powers. He did not make us in His own image in any physical way, but only in the very essential element of free will in the context of a meaningful life.

We have now arrived at the essential problem: In Chapter One, we concluded that the issue of pain and suffering is the foremost creation problem; it is linked in time and concept to creation itself;

and nothing proved more difficult for God than creating us. The story of Adam and Eve sets forth the parameters of that problem. How does Almighty God create beings in His own divine image? How can it be done? If He chooses to create beings of free will and meaning and choice, how can they live in Paradise where no meaningful choices exist? It is easy for us to say God should have created us in a heavenly garden, but if I were God how would I do it? Each being created there would be the same as every other. There would be no significant differences between any such beings and no beings of significant meaning.

The problem with Paradise is that we cannot actualize there as unique individuals of value and worth. The problem with free will and choice is that God must step back and give us space if we are to freely choose. Understanding the difference between good and evil is not so much a matter of original sin as it is a necessary condition of being human. It is the only way for us to decide what we want to be, and to have a life worth living with human dignity and intrinsic value.

In Paradise there is no risk and nothing to learn or to become. Every choice leads to happiness and choice itself becomes meaningless. It is difficult to conceive how we would expect God to partake in such a hoax, a creation where His creatures would essentially be valueless nonentities, incapable of any complex relationship with Him. We can certainly imagine a grander God than that.

Thus, we begin to see that Dawkins is correct in his observations, but faulty in his conclusions. An indifferent world is not a sign that He abandoned us, but that He created us. It is a conclusion drawn from the fact that God cannot interact with us in His own form if we are going to become or remain "us." The only way for God to create us as real individuals, is to build a wall of separation between us and Him.

And so it is that Chesterton in his spiritual journey came to recognize this also:

> "It was the prime philosophic principle of Christianity that this divorce in the divine act of making (such as severs the poet from the poem or the mother from the new-born child) was the true description of the act whereby the absolute energy made the

world. According to most philosophers, God in making the world enslaved it. According to Christianity, in making it He set it free."[4]

And so, let us return for a moment to the intuitive observations of some of our scientists from Chapter One. Recall that Carl Sagan pronounces that a Creator has nothing to do; Einstein came to admit that maybe God does play dice with the universe; Liebniz claimed that God had created the best possible universe; and Voltaire would ridicule Liebniz with the query "what must the others be like?" Is it possible that we can now see an answer to all of these diverse ideas? Is it possible that one vessel can navigate all these rivers?

If free will requires separation from God, can we not say that God has achieved this necessary separation? If He plays dice with the universe, is it because He does not care, or is it because He has let us go and the separation is real? Is it that the Creator has nothing to do, or is it that the Creator has chosen to do nothing?Can science ever discover exactly how creation began or is it that we are not meant to know, a final veil of separation that allows us to be absolutely free? If this is not the best possible world, then maybe C. S. Lewis is right: 'it is the only possible one where men and women of freewill exist.'[5] Thus Stephen Hawking, in addressing the anthropic principle mentioned earlier, answers Voltaire, "although (other universes) may be very beautiful, (they) would contain no one to wonder at that beauty."[6]

Therefore, in considering the facts and circumstances presented to us by science and by our own subjective review of our condition, the most plausible explanation of our pain and suffering comes from this idea of the necessity of separation from God at creation in order to imbue humanity with great numbers of unique individuals with dignity, value, and meaning. This problem was confronted by the mind and heart of God at the very conception of the universe.

From that point forward, we have been on a collision course with danger and death, but we have also been afforded the possibility of a relationship with God that is based upon and rooted within that dignity, value, and meaning.

This is the value of the Tree of Knowledge of Good and Evil. It is the pivotal point of understanding in the story of Genesis. This aspect of humanity – this element of free will within the context of a meaningful life of understanding and self-awareness – is more important than any other in all of Creation.

This idea is beautifully and poignantly depicted by the iconic painting of Michelangelo in the Sistine Chapel. In it, we see the outstretched hands of God and Adam reaching toward each other. Their fingers are almost touching, but between them remains a small, but distinct, separation. The space between them may be only inches, but, for us, it represents the separation of an entire universe and 13.7 billion years in time. All there is, or ever was, in the universe is contained within that space between their fingers.

This truly is a logical, remarkable creation and its magic can begin to be seen. We are part of and the focus of an extraordinary plan. We are perfectly positioned to fulfill our intended purpose as beings capable of relationship with the Almighty. The best God can logically create. What greater gift or greater purpose could there be?God cannot create other gods or lesser gods. To do so is a logical impossibility that diminishes the existence of one true, all-powerful God.

Even angels have their logical imperfections. They are comets in the sun. They may be spiritual beings without our physical limitations, but they are too close to God. Their light is not distinguishable; their will too easily overwhelmed by the sheer presence of God. In the Bible, they are typically seen as nothing more than extensions of God, as his messengers. Worse yet, Adam and Eve are mere, still-life paintings. They are devoid of truth and separated from meaning. They are unable to stand on their own two feet and in no real sense have the opportunity to choose God for themselves, of their own volition unencumbered by the presence of God's overwhelming spirit. They could never understand the joys of giving, or accomplishment, or love in so many of its forms. They would have no understanding of sorrow, loss, forgiveness, or redemption. They are empty shells without any true vestiges of Humanity.

Mankind, however, may be the perfect creation of a perfect God. It is a perfect plan grounded in logic and necessity, the best that could be conceived and it is executed by the Creator in all of His glory, by the Almighty Architect, Engineer, and Artist. To put it another way, original sin is not in man, but is in his condition. We have not fallen from Paradise, but we cannot live there. We did not bite the apple, but the apple is in our blood.

God, therefore, did not forbid the fruit of the Tree of Knowledge of Good and Evil from Adam and Eve simply to demand obedience. It was forbidden because complete innocence is a necessary condition for our state of being in Paradise. To exist in Paradise is to forego the will. In Paradise, everything is provided, and choice is of no consequence.

In order for us to exist, to fully self-actualize, we must be separated from Paradise and from God. Adam and Eve, therefore, did not cause our suffering by one solitary act. Suffering arises as a result of creation. We were created by the grace of God, and in His wisdom the indifferent environment of our universe alone can sustain us. In some sense, there was no universal fall of man. There was a rise, an evolutionary rise from nothingness. A coming of age. A crossing of the line. A biting of the apple. From pre-human to sentient being to choice; from choice to individualism; from individualism to the summit of ultimate decision – confronting the will of God. We walk a rising road. And if the fall exists, it exists in the individual and not the species. It exists in the condition with which we have to contend and in the antagonism between forging one's will and confronting God's.

The creation of Humanity removed from Paradise, as a concept, is perfect. Before there can be a Paradise we can enjoy and in which we can partake, we must first be beings of self-awareness and will. God did not create a harsh and indifferent world because He prefers that type of world. He did not create it to bring goodness out of evil. He did not create it to humble us or to cause us pain. He did not create it to punish us or to remind us to pray to Him.

God created this world and this universe as He did: Harsh and indifferent, with pain, with suffering, with tragedy and death, because He had no choice to make it otherwise. It is logically impossible for God to create Paradise, and at the same time, endow it with a population of beings who are self-aware and possess the gift of free will.

One cannot exercise free will in the immediate presence of God. His will, His power, and His light are overpowering, withering, overwhelming. We would be completely subsumed.

In order for Humanity to flourish as the perfect creation it is intended, a separation from God is completely necessary and logically impossible to circumvent. Paradise was lost in the very idea of Humanity. When God, our Father, created us, He knew He was letting us go.

> *"God looked at everything he had made, and he found it very good.*
> *'Evening came, and morning followed---the sixthday."*
> *Genesis 1:31*

Chapter Four
OUR FATHER WHO ART IN HEAVEN

Our Father in heaven,
Hallowed be your name, Your kingdom come,
Your will be done
On earth as it is in heaven.
Matthew 6:9-10

The Lord's Prayer: It tells us concisely and beautifully exactly how we need to pray. If we examine it a little more closely, it also reminds us of a few elemental truths. As we saw in Chapter Three, it is necessary for God to separate Himself from us in order to honor the gift of free will He has graciously given us.

The opening phrase of His son's prayer reminds us that God is in heaven and not on earth; that there is indeed this separation between us. A separation manifested in an indifferent world that is essential to the development of free will. However, pain and suffering result from that indifference too, and become an unfortunate and unavoidable byproduct of it. As we shall soon see, however, pain and suffering, unfortunate as they are, also provide the means to our salvation. It affords an opportunity to relate to and reunite with our God.

In the aftermath of tragedy, we reflexively ask where God is. We seek Him then and we wonder why. More often than not, we are left with the feeling that some things cannot be explained, and in faith we move on. The reality is that our human condition, predicated on freedom, prevents God from intervening systematically in our affairs.

Free will requires neutrality. Even the gentle coercion of God's love would be enough to unduly influence our choices and limit our growth as free individuals. To the extent that He intervenes directly in our lives to prevent evil and promote good, then we are inexorably bent to His will - not by our choice, but by our interest, like a dog to his master. In time, we lose our will and find we have little left to guide us but mere instinct. The more that He intervenes, the closer we are to Paradise, but the further we are from choosing Paradise ourselves.

The problem is: We cannot relate to God if we can't say no to Him. There must be a dynamic tension between two beings as a precondition of a fuller relationship. Each must be able to stand apart and stand alone. A relationship based on need is not true. Only when a relationship is based upon full and mutual election, can there be love and a surrendering of the will, a joining of souls, a marriage.

Of course, it cannot be said that a relationship with God is a relationship among equals, but it is a real relationship based on mutual election. The possibility of such a relationship is indeed a miracle in itself. It is a relationship where He has already accepted us. It is we who have the choice. God went through all of the effort of creating the universe, not only to create us (which He could have done as spiritual beings in heaven), but to create us in separation from Himself so that the choice is ours. Imagine yourself a pet lover who has gone through great effort and creativity to construct a beautiful home and grounds for yourself and a pet, but instead of picking out a pet yourself, you must wait until a pet comes to your door, rings the bell and selects you.

So, it is with God. We can accept Him. We can reject Him. This is only true because of separation, the miraculous idea that Almighty God would dare to allow Himself to be rejected. Paradise Lost is not a failure of Man. It is a miracle of God. C. S. Lewis saw this as "the most astonishing and unimaginable of all the feats we attribute to Deity."[1] The miracle is we are created in such a fashion that we are allowed to say no to God. It is the magic that creates the possibility of a real, complex relationship, but it is paid for by the separation that causes pain and suffering here on earth.

Our Father who art in Heaven . . .

We seek God, but we cannot find Him here. Here, on earth, we have to find ourselves; that is our mission. It is the intent of God's creation. Once developed and once actualized, God then becomes possible for us. We can relate to Him and we can choose Him.

Once we choose Him, embrace Him, righteously from love and not from interest, then we live in the fullness of His earthly creation.

Not only will the beauty and the bounty of this indifferent world surround us, but purpose and meaning as well. Thus, we are called to action by the next part of the prayer taught to us by Jesus, *"your kingdom come, **your will be done on earth** as it is in heaven"*.

In the meantime, He patiently waits for us to make that choice. He endures our travails with us. In the interim, we should not blame Him for having the choice. We should not blame Him for the risk of pain and suffering that forges the possibility of that choice. Our environment was carefully prepared and created with the neutrality and indifference necessary to nurture us into substantive beings. Beings who can stand alone, search for another and, in so doing, even further define and perfect, shape and create themselves.

How is it that we can arise out of the gift of separation from God and arrive at a point where we can create our individual selves and choose God?

In some larger sense, it is an evolution from the physics of the Big Bang and the biology of Darwin, billions of small steps in time away from the creation and the Creator. So far away, in time and understanding, that uncertainty becomes the essence of that wall of separation (i.e., we really don't know how we were created or whether God exists).

But in an individual sense, we arrive at that point of decision as a result of a long period of childhood incubation. "More than any other creature, human beings are able to change,"[2] says Alison Gopnik, professor of psychology at the University of California, in her book The Philosophical Baby. "A single unified self is something we create – not something we are given," she concludes.[3]

We are born as strangers into this world, helpless and completely dependent. Over time, we learn the ways of this world and how to define ourselves in it. This is no easy task. Though we choose incrementally and daily who we are and who we will be, it cannot be done in a vacuum. Everything that we have, and everything that we are, comes from the outside. What we learn, we learn from that which surrounds us. It therefore becomes important to reflect on the necessity of the other in defining ourselves.

So much of what we learn comes from the other—other things, other people, other situations. We are dependent upon the other for everything: life, sustenance, nurturing, relationship, and even, as we shall see, free will. The other is the environment that forms us and teaches us what we can be. The other is a forum for choice and rejection. We emulate who and what we wish to be and learn to discard or avoid what we dislike.

From infancy, we learn something about ourselves when we touch and feel other things. We also learn what we are not. When the opportunity presents itself, I challenge you to take a good look at an infant between six and twelve months old. This infant will teach you all about the other. Everything she does is in response to the other. She will look all around. She will stare. She will touch and grab and reach. This child may hit or throw or taste a nearby object. She may pull someone's hair or rip their eyeglasses off of their face. She will mimic, repeat, chase, and ignore. This child will use all of her energy to explore her surroundings and she will express joy, wonder, or frustration as she attempts to understand them and what they mean to her. This is the method of growth and development that we employ: trial and error, live and learn.

Our physical world manifests itself to us in those tactile and sensual ways as we explore our surroundings throughout our childhood. In a sense, that experience never stops. It continues ever onward as we grow and develop. This is due because of, and along with the other, the concept of all phenomena which are not me. It is exactly what C. S. Lewis means when he says that we meet no ordinary people in our lives.[4] We are all unique and extraordinary people finding our own way in this soul-making factory, which is our universe.

As it turns out, this process is even richer and more complex than we might imagine. The psychology of childhood development is quite revealing. In her book, Gopnik explores the capacity of small children, from the time they are infants to about the age of five-years-old, to learn, imagine, and love.

Children of this age group are intensely focused on the other, and they have a greater capacity to understand and connect than we realize. "The evolutionary imperative for babies is to learn as much as they can as quickly as possible. Their job is to make accurate (mental) maps of the world around them. They learn and infer, make causal maps (connections) and draw counterfactual (alternative) conclusions, and they don't need to worry if what they learn is relevant to some particular plan or goal."[5]

As a result, *"Babies seem to be conscious of much more of the world at once…they are picking up information about all of the objects around them, especially when that information is new. This capacity for very general attention makes babies and children such terrific learners… This lets babies and children construct new maps, and change their old ones, much more quickly and easily than adults do."*[6]

As babies, we are born into the world of the other. Everything we will come to know, we will learn from that world. In our early years, we are immersed in a prolonged and open study of this otherness. As the author points out, we are able to do so because we have an evolutionary advantage. We have evolved to allow a protracted period of "protected immaturity" in which "the drive to experiment seems to be innate…(and) provides us a way of learning things that are not innate."[7] This innate drive, therefore, provides us with a lifelong method of encountering the world and adapting to it; a process uniquely useful in the development and exercise of free will.

And so, the world of the other, physical and psychological, emotional and imaginative, completely draws us in and engages us as very small children. For the very young, it is a great adventure that we, as adults, have long ago forgotten. It especially includes the imaginative and gives no special preference to the real. It encompasses the entirety of the other and has yet to be narrowed into the sharper focus of adulthood.

As Gopnik puts it:

"From the adult perspective, the fictional worlds are a luxury. It's the future predictions that are the real deal. For young children, however, the imaginary worlds seem just as important and appealing as the real ones. It's not, as scientists used to think, that children can't tell the difference between the real world and the imaginary world… It's just that they don't see any particular reason for preferring to live in the real one."[8]

It is this total immersion in the other that explains so much of what children do and need. Children act the way they do, says Gopnik,

> "...because they are designed to rapidly and accurately learn the causal structure of the physical and psychological worlds around them...methods of experimentation and statistical analysis seem to be programmed into our brains even when we are tiny babies. Very young children unconsciously use these techniques to change their causal maps of the world. These programs allow babies, and so the rest of us, to find the truth."[9]

In a nutshell, Gopnik's book, and the vivid experiments and studies it is based upon, tells us that we encounter the other purposefully and with innate tools to do so from a very early age; very young children are dynamic learning machines open to all possibilities; they learn not only about things, but properties, how to predict results and analyze probabilities, processes that help them understand causes and manipulate their environments, processes that allow them to imagine alternatives, adapt quickly, and change in the light of new information.

Eventually, therefore,

> ". . . a child's early experiences can lead to a cascade of causal interactions that result in an adult with a particular character...those early experiences can lead to a cascade of successive theories that result in an adult with a particular view of the world. None of these relations are deterministic."[10]

Through this open-eyed awareness of the other, infants and children become more knowledgeable about the world. Eventually, that which was once new, becomes tried and true. Our focus shifts from learning to acting. At the other end of this stage of open-eyed awareness and initiation, we emerge as more sculpted adults, whittled down by the choices and experiences we have made and had in relationship to the other. We have become more focused on a narrow path of choice, interest, character, and personality than we have ever

81

been before. We have reached a certain understanding of the other now and we will change less in response to it.

But we have come a long way to reach this point and many possibilities were open to us. We are necessarily unique. The other has molded us, but we have found our own way through the particular environment into which we were born, and we have done so in the most wondrous way possible— in childhood.

Our interactions, relationships, and experiences define us. In a profound way, they are tools to the construction of our individual beings, especially from a purely personal perspective. Therefore, in order to answer the question of how it is that we can arise out of the gift of separation from God and arrive at a point where we can create our individual selves and choose God, we can say the following: God created the entire universe and every person in it directly for me as a tool to build myself. From each individual's perspective, it must always seem this way.

As we continue to explore the relationship between pain and suffering and creation, we must always recall that they are joined; the creation of this universe has a purpose, and pain and suffering are unavoidably intertwined with that purpose. We must be clear in our understanding that pain and suffering are born of the need of the Creator to separate Himself from His creation in order to give room for humanity to grow and develop in a meaningful way.

Thus, it can now be said, with the introduction of the concept of the other as necessary and vital to the development of the individual, that this universe was created by God for me and for me alone. We live in a self-centric universe.

But every individual has the same perspective, and they are all correct. God created us all for the unique development experience of the other. We are both subject and object in this quest. Uniquely alone and supremely important in one's own journey, the individual is also one of countless resources at the disposal of others on the same journey.

This gives us another insight into God and our relationship with Him. Not only is it necessary that God not directly intervene in our world in any systematic way, but it is also important that He finds a means to do so in some way. For that is the purpose of creation in the first place: To establish a meaningful, cognizant, fully actualized relationship between God and each individual. Separation is simply the means.

The most impressive thing to me about God's design is not the powerful lightning bolts, but the gentle rain, the use of millions or billions of small drops to water the earth. This motif is repeated throughout the universe. It is the concept of using the small in great numbers. It is brilliantly effective.

God interacts with us in much the same way. As we have noted, He cannot come to earth and solve our problems. He cannot prevent our tragedies and stay true to the concepts and purposes of creation. Yet, He is our Father. Though, from my own personal perspective, the rest of the universe and all of its people are my womb, God honors that perspective for each of us. We all have that unique opportunity to actualize, and today nearly eight billion of us are in the process of doing so simultaneously.

How then, can He help us without intervening in a way that diminishes us? The most effective and satisfying answer to that question is—the other. The most poignant example of this (that I have yet encountered) is found in a book written by Francis Collins, The Language of God. In it, he describes an encounter with a young Nigerian farmer. As the tale unfolds, we find that Collins has volunteered to relieve, for a short while, some missionary physicians in a small mission hospital in Nigeria. He describes his trepidation over his dependence on high-tech medical tools, which were nonexistent at his small facility, but he really felt he could make a difference while he was there.

Before long, he became depressed over the unavailability of proper resources and the inadequacy of the entire health care system in that region. He no longer felt that he could make much of a difference and he grew more discouraged daily.

He goes on to tell of this young farmer who came to see him one day. It quickly became apparent that the young man had accumulated a large amount of fluid in the pericardial sac around his heart, a life-threatening occurrence probably brought about by tuberculosis.

Collins realizes that the only way to save him was to draw out the fluid with a large needle. Collins recounts the rest of the story as follows:

> "In the developed world, such a procedure would be done only by a highly trained interventricular cardiologist, guided by an ultrasound machine, in order to avoid lacerating the heart and causing immediate death.
>
> No ultrasound was available. No other physician present in this small Nigerian hospital had ever undertaken this procedure. The choice was for me to attempt a highly risky and invasive needle aspiration or watch the farmer die. I explained the situation to the young man, who was now fully aware of his own precarious state. He calmly urged me to proceed. With my heart in my mouth and a prayer on my lips, I inserted a large needle just under his sternum and aimed for his left shoulder, all the while fearing that I might have made the wrong diagnosis, in which case I was almost certainly going to kill him."[11]

Luckily, for all concerned, the procedure was successful and though Collins was both relieved and elated, those feelings soon passed as he considered the prospects for this young man's life.

> "The chance for long life in a Nigerian farmer are poor. With those discouraging thoughts in my head, I approached his bedside the next morning, finding him reading his Bible...But then, this young Nigerian farmer, just about as different from me in culture, experience and ancestry as any two humans could be, spoke the words that will forever be emblazoned on my mind: 'I got the sense that you are wondering why you came here,' he said. 'I have an answer for you. You came here for one reason. You came here for me.'"[12]

Collins was stunned by the insight of this poor farmer. For in one brief moment, this farmer looked into the depths of the creation problem and understood the purpose of the universe. "You came here *for me."* God has designed a self-centric universe. This is God's plan, and Collins immediately understood it.

> *"He was right. We are each called to reach out to others. On rare occasions that can happen on a grand scale. But most of the time it happens in simple acts of kindness of one person to another. Those are the events that really matter... for just that one moment, I was in harmony with God's will, bonded together with this young man in a most unlikely but marvelous way."[13]*

This young man understood that all the universe was made for him. He understood that his life was valuable, and all kinds of tools were placed at his disposal, including even poor Mr. Collins. How fortunate for the young man that poor Mr. Collins was also in a time and place where he could use the young man for his own development. How fortunate for Mr. Collins that the young man could teach him an invaluable lesson.

Both of these men have found the universe a place to live and grow. Both of them are the richer for it. And life goes on. The factory of souls continues its work. The miracle of creation continues, and today nearly eight billion of us engage the other simultaneously in a self-centric universe to produce the souls that may one day choose to bond with God.

Your will be done on earth . . .

God intervenes in our world every day. He does so, not by His will or His act, but by the will and acts of others. Like the gentle raindrops that refresh the earth one by one, His children help each other every day.

The most fervent wish of any dying parent, of any soul on its way to heaven, is that his or her children and those he or she has left behind will take care of each other. It is the same for Our Father.

Chapter Five
THE GREATEST OF THESE IS LOVE

Herein is love, not that we loved
God, but that He loved us."
1 John 4:10

Imagine yourself at a special music concert given by your favorite artist, or as an audience member at one of your favorite Broadway shows. You have circled the date, invited a friend, bought the tickets, and keenly anticipated the evening. After several weeks, the date of the concert or show arrives. You meet your friend for dinner, and you drive to the event. Everyone is beginning to arrive, and the low buzz of conversation, laughter, and people on the move heighten your senses. There is an excitement in the air and a warm feeling in your heart. At last, the lights are dimmed, and the event begins. For a time, you are carried away and transported to another world. The performance is brilliant, even better than you had hoped. By night's end your emotions have been engaged, your energy released and your spirit renewed.

For me, the event might be a classical symphony or concerto, perhaps by Beethoven or Rachmaninoff - two of my favorites. I have had the good fortune to attend several great concerts over the years. The imagination of the composer, the artistry of the conductor, and the skill of the musicians combine to produce some of the most astounding moments possible for the human spirit. As one leaves such a performance, it is impossible not to feel uplifted and connected along with the rest of the audience.

This bit of joy may linger for several days. The sense of beauty, power, and communication present in great artistic performances wonderfully describes some essential aspect of the human condition, which we vaguely embrace in these moments. On some level, beyond the visceral enjoyment and pleasure, one is sure to feel a sense of pride in the individuals who produced such transcendent art. Indeed, one may feel a sense of pride in humanity itself at these moments.

We are capable of reaching great heights and it is good to recognize it when we can.

As sublime as all this can be, a different perspective may sometimes emerge long after the concert ends. As good as "the best we have ever seen" may be, it is sometimes deflating to consider that it must be entirely trivial and boring to God. It is sad to think that the best mankind has ever produced, or could ever produce, is, in itself, utterly inconsequential to God. Though it be written and performed with all the talent, effort, and skill possessed of any artistic genius, the work could not possibly be interesting to the Almighty.

This is a depressing thought. Sooner or later, we must ask ourselves, what need has God of us? It is undeniably true: God can outperform us in everything we do. He can make it better, faster, more efficiently, and more beautifully. He can do it as an act of will. There is nothing we can build, or create, or produce that He cannot do better Himself. Even though we were to produce them with love from the depths of our souls, our creations, in and of themselves, have no utility to God.

This is, of course, no great revelation. God is God, and we are but mere mortals. This difference between us creates a dilemma. How do mere mortals possibly hope to relate to their God? As small children, we may have given gifts to one of our parents on some special occasion. Perhaps it was handmade: a painted rock, clay figure, or decorated box, and perhaps we were immensely proud of it. Even so, it is unlikely to be found on the mantel or framed and hung in the living room. If we were to somehow stumble across those gifts today, youthful pride would give way to bewildered amusement. The tattered item would be nothing more than a humorous reminder of childhood innocence. Though they may have been kept and even cherished by the parent, it is now plain to see that they never were as useful as we may have intended them to be. Though children grow to adulthood and reach some parity with their parents, human beings never attain this with God. How then do we explain ourselves to God? It is an issue that is often overlooked, and one that we will consider momentarily.

To this point, we have explored God's creation and our place in it. Despite the awful scope of pain and suffering necessarily contained within the awesome beauty of our vast and indifferent universe, we have a better sense of what that pain and suffering represents – a byproduct of our separation from God which is necessary for the existence of our free will. We need no longer recoil in fear and horror from grisly or hopeless loss. We need no longer despair and question God's inaction or indifference.

We have learned that, in separation, we have been afforded the opportunity to say no to God and thus have been fully afforded the real opportunity to say yes – to encounter our God in a real relationship of give and take, of choice and true meaning.

As a consequence of this understanding, we need no longer despair and question God's inaction or indifference. More than ever before, we can reaffirm that our God is awesome in His power and awesome in His love. We can assent to the bold proclamation of Genesis that "it is good." To this point, it is possible to follow the logic and more clearly understand the problem of creation.

The issue we often overlook, however, is the reason for creating us at all. Being self-aware and acutely self-absorbed in this self-centric universe, we accept our existence and ponder our destiny, but give almost no thought at all to the motives of the Creator in bringing us forth. Why did He do it? What need does God have of us?

It seems very clear and easy to say that He has none. Maybe this is why the question is not often addressed. However, it is oddly amusing that we rarely even think of it. In this way, we take our existence for granted.

As mentioned in Chapter One, the most intuitive answer is our initial creation must have something to do with love. Mankind has long defined God as a creator and as a being of pure love. It seems natural that these attributes are intertwined. Our own experiences of love show that love is a creative force. It produces children, sustains families, and undergirds civilization. It is a great motivator and deeply inspirational. It is also compelling and outward-looking. Love is that force which takes man out of himself and in search of another.

Love is enduring, refreshing, affirming, hopeful, merciful, and life giving. It is joyful, compassionate, and forgiving. It renews the soul and reawakens the senses. Even Nietzsche refers to it as an overflowing of the soul.[1] It begins at that moment when the heart takes leave of the body. It has inspired poetry, letters, music, sculpture, painting, courage, heroism, altruism, and many of our finest qualities.

Love is a universal characteristic and feeling understood and desired in all places and at all times. In God, it is perfected, and it exists in the highest order possible. To comprehend the magnitude of God's love is, of course, impossible. Even though we are given an extraordinary example of it in the life of Jesus, we are not remotely capable of comprehending how it is that God loves. We must simply satisfy ourselves with the idea that it could not be surpassed. Despite these limits, it is possible to examine aspects of God's love as far as our minds will carry us. In order to do so we must examine the nature of God in so far as we can understand it.

Let us consider, for a moment, what it means to say that "I AM" and to hear the voice of God:

'I AM, a self-existent being, without any limits, save those which I may impose upon myself. I am every conceivable perfection in the highest possible order. I have no fear. I am incorruptible, impassable, indivisible, immense, fully and eternally actualized. I am one, complete, omniscient, unity. I am the source and perfection of all that is good. I am omnipotent. I am, therefore, incapable of fear. As such, my omnipotence cannot corrupt me or tempt me. For I will do what I choose and what I choose is always good, for I am and it pleases me. Only the fearful are corruptible, for their fear makes them vulnerable. Without fear, I am free to love and trust without limit.

You have heard that absolute power corrupts. On earth this appears to be true, but only because no one holds such power. Were one to hold it, no corruption could exist. Corruption and temptation are both born of fear. Even the most powerful of your kings or dictators have much to fear. Their power is limited and temporary and will one day leave them. This they know. It is this that they fear. It is the fear that corrupts them. But, I AM. And fear will never know me. And love is mine and it rests upon my power and it flows freely from me.'

God exists in utter self-fulfillment and His being crowds out or presupposes all other existence. A God of power and might and complete self-sufficiency can have no deficiencies and no needs. Thus, once again, we have found God where He is, and it is a place where He has no need of us. But it is also a place where He is free to love completely and infinitely.

From what we can surmise of the immutable nature of God, He is free to love, encompasses all love that is good and loves in a fashion that befits His nature. This love is an unimaginable force. We have seen glimpses of it in His creation. As alluded to earlier, it is such an imponderable wonder that it would even induce the Almighty to suffer rejection at the hands of the creatures He has made but doesn't need. Like poor Mr. Goodman, who we earlier left building a grand estate for a prospective pet, He has found that no pet will accept Him, or worse, that the ones who come to knock on His door, move in and ignore Him. It is an extraordinary matter, this love of God's.

We need not further pursue the nature of God so directly, a weighty endeavor that would take us far afield of our task. But on this quest to understand this God of ours – the God who allows our pain and suffering – it is necessary to consider our predicament from His perspective. We cannot begin to do that without seriously reflecting on His nature to some extent.

On the other end of the spectrum, we have human love. Where the love of God is unlimited and unending, human love is imperfect and inconsistent. It must always fight the sometimes-selfish urge of being and becoming oneself in this self-centric universe.

Our journey through life is uniquely focused on self as we seek to define, uncover or reassert who we are. It is a vestige of our humanity that we are at times wholly self-absorbed in this endeavor. In other moments, we can step far outside the boundaries of self and encounter a wider vision of growth and development. If love succeeds, then we may find ourselves lost in another and becoming a new self. The self-centric universe can be transcended.

In speaking of human love, we might examine what it is not. It is not the opposite of hate. The antithesis of human love is not hatred. Hatred stems from the frustration of failing to (or being prevented from) achieving or maintaining one's self-image. One may come to hate oneself or another when one's identity is threatened.

Though I were to be killed or maimed by an intruder, I may well feel pride, even in death, if I died defending my home, family or country. My self-mage is affirmed - even at a cost I'd rather not pay. The rest of my family may well indeed feel anger and hatred, for their circumstances are different. The ways they define themselves are now forever changed. It is a frustration that does not easily depart. On the other hand, were this same intruder merely to call me a coward or publicly insult me and impugn my character, I may well learn to hate the one who challenges my pride – my self-image.

Hatred stems from the perception that there is a lack of acceptance, respect, and commonality with another. It breeds indifference and can flare into anger if lines are crossed. It is based on a great lack of understanding and a cold carelessness. If left unchecked, hatred pursues redress, vengeance and destruction. However, were hatred to pursue kindness, understanding and support, it would be called friendship. Thus, the opposite of hatred is more akin to friendship or common interest or connectedness.

So, it is not hate that usually obstructs or challenges love. Love is an opening up of oneself to another. It is allowing oneself to become vulnerable in the hopes that one's carefully crafted ego is ready to be successfully shared with another. Love will cause the self to risk being vulnerable. Yet, there is another emotion that will not risk it. The force that really obstructs or challenges love is fear. It is fear that prevents the seeds of love from taking root.

Where love wishes to jump out of its heart and participate in the world or pursue another, fear wishes to retreat into the self and construct formidable, protective defenses. It brings caution, but it can cause loss and missed opportunities.

How many times have we failed to pursue our hearts? How many dreams have drifted away?

What would have happened if I would have talked to her or asked her out?

Where would I be if I would have accepted that date, made that phone call, spoke from my heart?

How is it that I did not pursue the job, career or life that called out to me?

Few are the ones who have followed their dreams and their passions. Fewer still are the ones who regret having followed them. But even for them and for all the rest, it is fear that would stop them.

There are many fears, and we know them well: fear of failure, of rejection, of humiliation, of disapproval, of shame, of danger, of incompetence, of disappointment, of contempt, of confrontation, of broken hearts and wasted resources. Those fears and others may cause lack of confidence, low self-esteem, lack of courage, indolence, misguided actions, lowered expectations, exaggerated perceptions, pretensions and dishonesty. In turn, these attributes may lead to a lack of generosity towards others, unfair criticism, scorn, disapproval, intolerance, jealousy, ridicule and prejudice.

The problems of fear are many and formidable. They are inseparable from the instinct to protect the self and to proceed cautiously in all matters. Though we live in a self-centric universe, we stand and grow in opposition to it. We are bumped and bruised and sometimes beaten.

It is no accident that in some form or another, that the phrase "Do not be afraid," is recited over 20 times in the gospels. It seems to be the mantra of our Lord and is spoken many more times than the phrase "love one another." It is exceedingly difficult to get to love if fear is holding us back.

The basis and proof of human love, therefore, is letting go of fear. It is many things, but above all it is learning and willing to reach beyond the self, and ultimately to be willing to deny the self.

It is running into the burning building, falling on the grenade, fighting injustice, speaking the truth, following your heart, taking the blame, testing your limits, admitting your faults. Letting go of fear may be as simple as speaking in public or as difficult as fighting your demons. It may mean asking for help or consoling a stranger. It can come in the form of an offered hand, a kind word or a forgiving smile.

Human love is letting go of fear, of learning to lose oneself to gain something more. Like the creation of the universe, it has a vast richness about it. This one idea is manifested in so many ways. It is found in the Sermon on the Mount, in leading a just cause, in giving from need, or in breaking up a fight. Yet every step of the way, the shadows of fear color the light of love.

One of the brighter lights of love is the love of children. The great privilege and gift of parenting teaches many lessons of love. Though it is not without its great fears, the love born of raising children is more commonly linked to perseverance and the joy found in the gift of life.

One of the most extraordinary and courageous examples of perseverance and joy in parenting that I have ever heard is presented in the following true story. It is a moving and beautiful story, which encompasses so much of what human love is about.

35 Minutes to Live, Feel Love

Jessica and Dave Weatherford knew Zeke's time on earth would be mere moments. His birth would be filled with warmth and caring. Jessica Weatherford lies helpless on the operating table, staring at a blue surgical sheet hanging inches from her face. It blocks her view of the Caesarean on the other side, as a doctor reaches for her baby. A baby Weatherford has been waiting for. A baby she prays will live long enough to hold.

Weatherford, 29, feels nothing, hears nothing except her husband, Dave, 35, who is talking about two years earlier. Then, Weatherford had gone through an emergency Caesarean, deep anesthesia. It brought forth Victoria, 'Tori' Ann, now nearly 2.

This time she is awake, the C-section planned, but there is no question about the outcome. Their boy won't endure beyond the womb. Zeke, they have named him, short for Ezekiel, meaning 'God is my strength."

A tiny head appears. The doctor tugs, and between his hands a tiny head appears, covered in wet curls. Weatherford feels her husband's hand gripping hers. He's scared too,

93

Weatherford remembers her excitement in November when she saw an image of the 20-week fetus and the sonogram technician said it was a boy. Then the technician grew quiet, and when the Weatherfords saw the doctor, his face wore the news. 'I'm sorry,' he said. 'There are abnormalities with your baby's brain and abdomen. Problems too great to fix.'

More tests brought more bad news: His heart's veins and arteries were on the wrong sides. A sack containing half his organs was growing outside his body. Amniocentesis confirmed a non-hereditary birth defect: full trisomy 13.

Weatherford decided the best gift she could give to her unborn son was to love him until his death, even if the only fullness of his life would be in the soft cushion of her womb.

Many people wouldn't continue a doomed pregnancy. But for the Weatherfords, it was the right choice. Two weeks after the doctor's visit, a phone rang at the home of Patti Lewis in Kansas City, Missouri. On the line, a young woman cried and cried. "Everybody cries when they call here," said Lewis, 56, who has helped 200 families through her non-profit Alexandra's House, a perinatal hospice.

She opened the house to be a place of caring for families grieving the loss of any infant, be it an unexpected stillborn, a miscarriage, an abortion or an unborn baby the parents know won't survive.

Weatherford and her husband visited Alexandra's House. Lewis shared with them how other families loved their babies at death. Told them all the ways they could love Zeke to remember him forever.

That night Weatherford wrote in her journal that for the first time in weeks, she felt hope. Zeke's due date was five weeks away.

Soon a midwife asked the question Weatherford had been dreading: Had she decided on a vaginal birth or a Caesarean? "A Caesarean... Give you more time to enjoy your son," the midwife counseled gently.

Lewis reminded Weatherford that a birth plan would help control who would be in the delivery room and how they wanted Zeke's final moments to be. Lewis also told her about the arrangements a hospital could make for mothers whose infants die, like moving her into a room on a different floor, away from other mothers and their babies. When leaving the hospital, she could go out a different door, so she wouldn't have to see another new mom cuddling her baby. Weatherford nodded. She marked it all in her notebook.

At 1:30 a.m. March 6, a week before her C-section was scheduled, contractions began. At 4:10 a.m., Weatherford was admitted at Overland Park Regional Medical Center in Kansas. Lewis already was there. The sound of a thumping heart filled her room, 132 beats a minute: Zeke.

Outside, Weatherford's parents, Lori and Rick Singleton, had arrived. Rick Singleton's eyes were red rimmed. Nurses wheel Weatherford into the operating room. Her husband and the entourage wait outside while she got an epidural. Dave gathers everyone to pray. "Lord, this is your baby... We just pray that... we'll have time with Zeke... Amen."

The operating doors open and a nurse waves everyone in. Zeke's legs are moving as the doctor pulled him from Weatherford. It is 5:23 a.m. Zeke doesn't cry. His mouth, with a double cleft lip on either side, slowly opens and closes. He has no nose. Zeke's bluish skin begins to turn pink. Dave Weatherford places him in his wife's arms. "Hi," she whispers. "This is Mommy. I love you." With a finger she strokes his cheek, seeing only a tiny baby, fragile and pure, with a mop of curly hair. A baby who has touched so many lives. She kisses him. "Ohhhh," she coos, as if her lips had brushed against the smoothest silk. Each time she speaks, Zeke moves his head just a little, jostled his tiny hand just a little.

Two, then three, then four more masked faces enter the room. They crowd around the bed: Weatherford's twin sister, Jacquelyn; her father; her mother-in-law, Kathy Weatherford; her minister, Rex Bonar. Aunts. Grandparents. Friends. They hug each other, reach out to pat her. "Do you want some skin-

to-skin contact, Jess?" her husband asks. She nods. One tear rolls down her cheek, then another.

Dave Weatherford and a nurse pull sheets down so Zeke is lying on Jessica's sternum. She smiles at feeling his little body. But too soon, she realizes that Zeke is leaving. His cheeks turn sallow, then a shade of blue.

'No, no, no,' she cries.

"No, no, no," Weatherford cries. Softly at first, and then with a deep, sobbing grief, wails of pain. And every person moving or whispering or writing stops.

Dave Weatherford breaks down in his mother's arms.

To confirm what Jessica already knows, a doctor listens for life.

"He's done," the doctor says. The digital clock reads 5:58.

By Lee Hill Kavanaugh[2]

What an amazing gift life is. The beauty in this story is incredible. There is nothing more to add. Love is not always easy, but it is almost always amazing.

And so, we see that the depths of human love can be great, despite its obstacles. And we know that the love of God is greater still, is of the highest possible order, and quite inconceivable to us.

Notwithstanding our limitations, however, we do know something of love. We recognize its attributes, we live on its dream, and we sing and dance to its music. It may well be the most valuable commodity we have and the most essential part of our being. St. Paul recognizes it as the greatest of spiritual qualities, for it is everlasting. In heaven, faith is proven, and hope is fulfilled, but love remains.

So, what remains of the mystery of our creation? Why does He bother with us? In all that we know about love, we are right to attribute it to God and correlate it with His nature. Yet, despite these many qualities, which we so freely and so rightly associate with the concept of God and which are so often concomitant with the notion of creation and creative energy, it is not possible to simply say or infer that since God is love, that love is creative, that God has created us and, therefore, that He must create. Though it is possible to say many things about His nature, it is not possible to say that it is God's nature to create. Any concept of God must necessarily accept the idea that God is wholly self-contained and wholly self-sufficient. There can be no need to create and, therefore, it cannot be part of the nature of God as if it were a need.

To accept any other analysis is to diminish the character of God and to reduce His power, freedom, and being from almighty power and infinite freedom. If we are to take God seriously, we must recognize that such logic is faulty. To assert it is to assume that there are limits to God's will. It is a weak argument. It relies on the fact of our existence as the proof that God must create. In other words, He did create us, so He must create us. It does not follow.

The alternative conclusion, however, is somewhat frightening. The truth of the matter is that God has no need to create us, and He has no need for us. This is true by the very definition of God as one, complete, incorruptible, indivisible, infinite, unity. Despite the power of love fully invested in God, there is no need of us. Any amount of reflection on this point serves only to convince us of its veracity.

So, we return to the great mystery. How do we explain ourselves? Is our existence due to a whimsical stroke of luck? Do we entertain God? Are we an outlet for His love? What possible relevance do we have? Why does God need any children? There would seem to be nothing we can give Him or do for Him that He couldn't accomplish Himself. It really seems an impenetrable mystery.

In our attempt to address it, let us start with what we know: The one thing that must clearly be acknowledged is that our existence is dependent upon God's will. It is not the result of any necessity nor of any reflexive act, but of a choice that He made.

In making the choice, the constraints of logical necessity remain manifest. Once the choice is made, it must be done within certain logical parameters. These have been discussed earlier. In making the choice, all of the elements and attributes of love do come forth and are further evidence of the nature of God. However, it is not His nature that causes the choice.

We see His love at work. We see that in creating us free, we embody the possibility of love, but He must let us go. He must create a vast and indifferent universe for us, and we see the love and beauty in His creation. We have come to realize that He suffers with us as we complete our journeys. There is great love present in all of this. But in order to understand why He did this, we must step back and look at the whole picture.

First, He has no need of us.

Second, He created us.

Third, His creation is perfectly suited to His goal, but requires an environment of indifference and of separation from Him, which inevitably causes us pain and suffering, sometimes perceived by us to be a great evil.

Through faith we know He created us, and for the purposes of this book it is assumed that He created us. We know now of the limits and constraints necessary to create us as beings of intellect and free will, but why does He do it? Foolproof answers to questions like these are, of course, impossible. We are incapable of understanding our own decisions and motivations at times, let alone those of other human beings, much less those of the Almighty.

Still there must be some reason. We cannot assume God is frivolous. If we are here, there must be at least one reason, consistent with all of the concepts discussed previously. What is it then?

The best answer that can be given that is true to the nature and concept of God is that God, in His perfect, selfless wisdom, understands that beings in His presence would be afforded overwhelming, eternal joy.

He did it for us.

Chapter Six
THE BIG BANG

To my mind, there must be at the bottom of it all, not an utterly simple equation, but an utterly simple IDEA. And to me that idea, when we finally discover it, will be so compelling, and so inevitable, so beautiful, we will all say to each other, 'How could it have ever been otherwise?
John Wheeler, Theoretical Physicist

The cosmos could be larger, richer and more varied than anything we imagined.
Lisa Randall, Theoretical Physicist

Growing up Italian gives a person certain advantages. Though not a full-blooded Italian, three of my four grandparents were, and I always deeply appreciated identifying with my heritage and culture. Italy brings to life a wealth of tradition, history, language, art, music, invention, culinary delight, politics, religion, and every other aspect of culture, community and civilization.

Raised in the Chicago suburbs as part of an extended Italian family, I have very fond memories of my youth. As a young boy, I lived with my parents, brother, and sisters in an upstairs apartment above my grandfather, grandmother, and aunt. My grandparents, who were both born in Sicily, owned the house in which we lived. The house was a two-story brick structure built by my grandfather, who was a carpenter. Though located on a busy street, it had a big backyard with open spaces and many fruit trees.

Two uncles and two other aunts and their families all lived nearby. I was one of seventeen cousins who enjoyed growing up together while having fun and learning from one another. We came together often, and it was more or less expected that we would gather together at my grandparent's home on most Sunday afternoons or evenings for a meal or a visit. Every holiday was a must, and most birthdays too! There were weddings and anniversaries, picnics and celebrations.

Great aunts and uncles, family friends, and second cousins also added to the mix. It was not a quiet bunch, but it was a colorful blend of personalities and a wonderful way to grow up.

A snapshot in time from any of those gatherings would readily recall, for any family member, many of the warm memories and interactions that we shared. Recently, I had occasioned upon just such a scene in an old home movie. It was taken on Independence Day and depicted us in the middle of dinner around a long string of tables in the middle of the yellow brick patio behind my grandparent's house. It was an aerial shot: most of us were sitting at the table, some half-standing reaching across the table, and others walking about the group serving the pasta, salads, or other dishes. It's a remarkable moment, capturing the life of an active family, its relationships, antics, energy, and way of life.

It's no secret that Italians are sometimes depicted this way, gathered around a table, loud, energetic, and boisterous, enjoying each other, along with the wine, music and food. *Delicioso*.

From this picture (or at least from this general idea), it occurred to me that my family and Italians in general celebrate a great truth. There is a word, familiar enough, that seems to describe this concept rather well. The word is *abbondanza*. It is the Italian word for abundance, and it aptly describes the way Italians approach their meals. Never is there a shortage of food at an Italian dinner. There is always more: more vino, more antipasto, more insalate, more pane, more frutta, more verdure, more carne, more pesce, more biscotti, and more pasta... always more pasta. It is impossible to leave hungry, nor is it allowed.

In the days of my youth, I ate until I was stuffed only to discover that the meal was far from over. More was coming and I risked offending my grandmother if I didn't eat it all up. *"Mangia, Francesco. Mangia!"*

To make matters worse, the meals were absolutely delicious-- the best food, prepared in the Italian tradition (with love), by the best cooks. I didn't want to stop; it was just that I couldn't take another bite. *"Mangia, Francesco. Mangia!"*

It is not only a celebration of food, but of love, giving and togetherness. *Abbondanza*, the Italians know it well. It is this same concept that evidently bemuses God too. Like so many of the other ideas in this book, it is not from knowing the mind of God that we can make this inference, but simply from what we can observe.

Look at His creation. Stop for a minute and think about what He has created. Can it be claimed for even one second that anything was spared? - that anything was missing? We live in a universe that is even wilder than our wildest imaginations. We haven't even seen but a tiny fraction of it. Forget, for a moment how it all works. Forget the physics, the natural laws, or the incomprehensible structure of it. Focus simply on the sheer variety found in nature.

One has only to peruse the latest publications on astronomy to open one's mind to the imagination and creativity in this universe. We understand so little of it. How do we begin to comprehend what we could find in and among the 2 trillion galaxies science now estimates could exist in our universe?

Even in our own solar system, we are only just beginning to discover many of its wonders. How many of us have any idea of the number of moons in Saturn's orbit? Or in Jupiter's? The surprising answer is that there are over 160 of them. One of these moons is believed to have more water under its surface than earth contains on its surface. How many of us know that on Venus a day lasts longer than a year? How many were taught that the sun represents 99.86 percent of the mass of our solar system? How many of us had any idea that right now somewhere on Neptune it is raining diamonds?[1]

Here on earth, almost everything is a wonder unto itself. Let us briefly examine the topic of living organisms on our own planet: Not only are there animals, but there are all kinds: from the magnificent horse to the lowly aardvark. There are elephants and bears, wolverines and antelopes, zebras and musk ox. Recall the otter, the panther, or lynx. Remember the rabbit, the buffalo, and mink. Consider the giraffe and the baboon. Would you have ever thought of such a creature on your own? I am only scratching the surface.

If we narrowed down the animal kingdom to just the horse, what choices still remain! There is the Pinto, Palomino, Appaloosa,

Clydesdale, Thoroughbred, Morgan, Tennessee Walker, Arabian, American Quarterhorse, Brumby, Hungarian Shagya, Cob, Barb, Trakchner, Shire, Orlov, Friesian, Holstein, Danish, Lipizzaner, Percheron, Breton, American Saddle, Dutch Draft, Rhineland Heavy Draft, Standardbred, Mustang, Ardennais, Boulannais, Gelderland, Suffolk, Missouri Fox Trotter, Irish Draft, Schleswig, Hackney, Oldenburg, Brabant, Swedish Ardennes, Cleveland Bay, Anglo Arab, Hanoverian, Polish Arab, Waler and Groningan. We could go on. There is the Shetland, Dale, Fjord, Batak, and over twenty-five other breeds of ponies as well. As it is, we are only talking about animals.

Not only are there insects, but there are all kinds: from the industrious honeybee to the lowly mite.

Not only are there reptiles, but there are all kinds: from the ferocious crocodile to the placid iguana.

Not only are there amphibians, but there are all kinds: from the giant bullfrog to the subterranean salamander.

Not only are there birds, but there are all kinds: from the improbable pelican to the impeccable finch.

Not only are there fish, but there are all kinds: from the exotic lamprey eel to the beautiful blue marlin.

Not only are there crustaceans, but there are all kinds: from the skittish crab to the clinging barnacle.

Not only are there mollusks, but there are all kinds: from the gangly octopus to the imbedded oyster.

Not only are there all kinds of these organisms, but, in many cases, they come in astounding numbers. Fish fill the rivers, oceans and lakes, enough to feed the world. Imagine the numbers. Imagine the numbers before the modern world, before the discovery of the Americas. Think of the buffalo that roamed the Great Plains. At their peak, it was estimated that there were over 80 million of them. Thundering herds that could shake the earth when they ran.[2]

Similarly, we could move from complex organisms and discuss the variety and numbers of simple organisms. Perhaps you would rather skip over amoeba and bacteria and instead talk of trees?Coniferous or deciduous? If deciduous, would you prefer softwood or hardwood? The oak? What kind? There are pin oaks and white oaks, red oaks and bur oaks. There are the black oaks, swamp oaks, Arkansas oaks and Chapman oaks. There are also the post oaks, water oaks, lacey oaks, Durand oaks, and Mohr oaks. Should one care for more choices, then there are the chinkapin oaks, chestnut oaks, overcup oaks, English oaks, and southern red oaks. There are the turkey oaks, bear oaks, Georgia oaks, and blackjack oaks. Not quite satisfied? What of the northern red oaks, Shumard oaks, nut tall oaks, swamp chestnut oaks, swamp white oaks, or northern pin oaks?

Consider any other tree or flower. Consider the fruits, the grains, the grasses, or the seeds. Let's go back to my grandparent's house for a moment. On a modest half acre site, about fifty years ago, they kept a plum tree which bore the most delicious small yellow plums, an Italian plum tree, two pear trees, three varieties of concord grapes, an apricot tree, raspberry bushes, two mulberry trees, a blackberry bush, a vegetable garden, a rose garden, a flower garden, a long row of lilac bushes, and an old willow tree. We could play this game for a long time.

Does this planet bore you? This solar system? There are trillions more. There are more galaxies too, and perhaps more universes. If you are unimpressed by variety, then what of quantity? Will you have time in your life to explore all of the landscapes, all of the mountains, all of the oceans, or the plains, or the deserts, or the rivers, swamps, lakes, or valleys? Will you have time in your life to calculate the number of squirrels that scamper about this world?

If you are unimpressed even by quantity, then what of quality? What of complexity? What of engineering and structure? Are you impressed by immensity? Or beauty? Or history? What about imagination and the inner workings of the human mind? What about the study of behavior, mathematics, or of any science? This universe is vast and rich in comparison to our need. Though I am only pathetically able to convey this idea in words, think of the elegant manner in which God has done so in the creation that is all around us.

Abbondanza is the word for this. It is an incalculable embarrassment of riches. It is abundance beyond reason. God is so lavish in His giving; it is truly inconceivable to the mind. It is, of course, the immensity, beauty, variety and complexity of this world that compels us to consider the possibility of God in the first place. It is that awesome.

In this chapter, I am not concerned with how God created the universe. There are many intriguing theories about this, and science will continue on its scintillating journey with due determination. Whether creation occurred according to the theory of the Big Bang or due to a Multiverse or as explained by String Theory or some other concept, I do not know. I will leave it to brighter minds than mine to explore.

For one, I have already stated my presumption that God exists; therefore, God created everything that exists. It matters little to me the method of design that He chose. My concern is limited to resolving the problem of pain occurring in a creation presumed to be God's handiwork.

Secondly, though in all sincerity, I do not desire to disparage in any way the pursuit of science or of truth in any form as to this question or any other, it strikes me that even a moderately educated child knows that no scientific creation theory yet proposed solves anything concerning God. Science has evolved fantastic theories and incredible tools. They hold some truth and potentially enormous practical utility, but they tell us nothing of metaphysical importance.

Why are we here? How did the Big Bang begin? How do you create something out of nothing?

Where is the science that can answer these questions? Science presumes to talk about creation and evolution as if it had, or will discover, the source of all knowledge. Though its journey is fascinating, exciting and essential, science can never discover this. Science seeks to discover answers to the question "How?," but sooner or later "How?" blends into "Why?," and science reaches its end. Science may tell us there was a Big Bang or that there are an infinite number of universes, but it seems to be at a loss to say what ignited the big bang or who or what created the first universe.

If one steps back from the minutia of detail and the ecstasy of mathematical equation, it may be that the bigger picture has a tale to tell. The focus of this chapter is to examine what God has created and to fathom to what purpose such an incomparable design is suitable.

We find ourselves in the midst of an inconceivably, fantastic environment. It is rich, vast, beautiful, complex, evolving, enchanting, and inexhaustible. After thousands of years of human development, we have gained some impressive insights, but our level of understanding about most things is still rather primitive. Well into the 21st century, we have discovered and documented some 1.6 million species of plants and animals on earth. However, it is estimated that there are over 7 million more species we have yet to discover.[3] We are on an exciting adventure, but we have a long way to go.

As noted earlier, the sublime Chesterton finds God in this creation because it is all so overwhelming and affirming, yet at the same time so unexpected. Not only may we enjoy all of the remarkable beauty that one day could offer, to wit: a glorious sunrise dawning its soft, filtered, white light on a sparkling, dew-drenched meadow; the call of the morning dove; wispy white clouds in a blue sky greeting the morning glories and a doe at forest's edge; an afternoon storm, charged with electricity, blowing in from the mountain tops trailed by a rainbow; a blazing sunset of pink and purple hue; and the midnight moonbeams dancing to the music of the ocean's rolling waves… but, somehow, we get to do it all over again!? every single day!? And especially tomorrow!? It is much like the ecstatic child on Christmas morning being told that tomorrow will be Christmas too, and everyday thereafter. Where is the justice in this world if every day has such charms? How do we deserve all of this? How is it we can have it more than once? If this is an indifferent world, the deck may be stacked in our favor. Thus, Chesterton addresses the problem of pain with the problem of pleasure. If one appears unjust, then so does the other.[4]

Though I revel in Chesterton's perspective, I believe that there is even more to it. This concept of *abbondanza* isn't simply a balance to the problem of pain. Nor is it simply a reaching out by God to suggest His existence to us. It is more like a vast playground or a laboratory where we are given the opportunity to experiment and become whoever it is that we wish to be.

Once again the concept of free choice seems paramount in all of God's creation. The process of creating free will---of creating us in His image---not only requires an indifferent world, a world removed from God's immediate presence, but a world rich, vast and complex, full of every possibility.

If God is the perfect Creator, then He will create perfectly within the parameters of logical necessity. Whereas before, we examined the logical limitations of His creation necessitated by the goal of creating beings of free will, we can now examine the unbounded generosity of His creation; a creation which envelops us like a cocoon, serves to help us grow and fosters the idea that we have unlimited potential.

Though this may all be readily acknowledged, we must admit that we tend to lose ourselves in the daily demands of life. We take it all for granted, as if we are somehow entitled to it. How privileged we are when we can learn to ignore a sunset; when we do not notice the stars at night, nor the green grass; nor the autumn leaves.

Yet it is there and given. As author Annie Dillard states, "If the landscape reveals one certainty, it is that the extravagant gesture is the very stuff of creation."[5] This extravagance appeals on so many levels. It is a constant call to our souls, yet always with the dignity and importance of solemn silence.

Thankfully, there are those sublime moments in life when we are so overwhelmed by the gifts of creation that they are impossible to ignore. Some years ago, I was driving home from a softball tournament in central Illinois with my oldest child, Noelle. She was a player on a travel team, and I was one of the coaches. Those days were always time well spent together, but this was a particularly long, hot, and dusty weekend.

It was a late Sunday afternoon towards the very end of June. After a quick bite to eat, we were both glad to get on the road and head back home. As I recall, we were both tired and quiet as we travelled along. There is not much to grab one's attention driving through this part of the country in mid-summer. There was nothing but farms and their acres and acres of flat, green, growing fields.

About an hour into our ride, we noticed the sun going down and dusk settling in. We then first began to notice the sight that neither one of us will ever forget. As we drove along and the dusk darkened into night, fireflies by the tens of thousands began to rise up from the shallow heights of the bean fields. Acre after acre, mile after mile, as far as the eye could see on either side of the highway, these glorious little fireflies kept us company and awestruck on our journey. Their little yellow lights flickered on and off as we drove on for 50 or 60 miles. We must have seen millions of these luminous little gems twinkling in the summer sky. It was like passing through an incandescent garden. I don't believe Noelle and I even said a word about the astounding, mystical pageant we were witnessing. We didn't have to. Maybe we couldn't. It was sublime artistry of the highest order.

This vision rolled on for about an hour in the most impressive natural display I have ever seen. As we left the farm fields behind and regained the suburban light-scape, we lost sight of the fireflies. But we did get to hear the laughter of God and chuckle along with Him.

In a bit of extraordinary irony, our hometown's 4th of July fireworks were just going off as we neared our destination. Though we could see the bright colors in the sky and hear the explosions, it just could not compare to what we had already seen. All we could do now was to look at each other with the contented smiles of those who had experienced the grace of God. When we become too accustomed to the ordinary, we have spectacle to remind us. The great gifts of abundance are no accident.

In its quiet, respectful way the staggering abundance of the universe humbles us into thoughts of the divine. As proud as we are of our scientific endeavors, we sit as infants in contemplation of His work. He is the Great Giver, and this is basically the answer pointedly given by God in the Book of Job to silence His critics.

The utilization of free will is one thing. The creation of it is quite another. The Book of Job addresses the enormity and difficulty of this undertaking. It seems to realize that creating free will is a complex and multifaceted problem that only God can resolve.

Without resolving the problem of pain and suffering, the Book of Job does, at least, raise the issue directly. Its obtuse answer to the problem centers on the fantastic power and imagination required to create an environment where free will can flourish.

Thus, when God is interrogated about the unjust sufferings of Job, He admonishes His detractors and speaks to them of creation:

> "Where were you when I founded the earth? Tell me, if you have understanding, who determined its size; do you know?... Have you ever in your lifetime commanded the morning and shown the dawn its place...Have you ever entered into the sources of the sea or walked about in the depths of the abyss? ...Tell me, if you know all: which is the way to the dwelling place of light and where is the abode of darkness ...You know, because you were born before them and the number of your years is great! ...Can you raise your voice among the clouds, or veil yourself in the waters of the storm? Can you send forth the lightnings on their way, or will they say to you here we are?...Do you know about the birth of the mountain goats, ...Will the wild ox consent to serve you?... Do you give the horse his strength? ... Does the eagle fly up at your command?...Will we have arguing with the Almighty by the critic? Let Him who would correct God give answer!"
>
> *Job, Ch 38 – 40.*

At first blush, God's retort to Job and his friends clearly conveys the idea that God is the powerful one in this debate, and if His critics cannot match the power or comprehend the ingenuity of His creation, then they have no right to even be in this conversation.

> "Who is this that obscures divine plans with words of ignorance?"
>
> *Job 38: 2*

To say the least, God seems to be indignant with his accusers. Though Job, an upright man, has suffered greatly, a lack of humility pervades the criticisms thrown out to God. Though God clearly questions their integrity in this debate, it is squarely based on their ignorance.

From my perspective, the inference that can be drawn from God's reply is that we have no idea of the difficulty involved in creation. We neither understand the goals of creation nor its mechanics. We do not comprehend the difficulty involved in creating the appropriate environment for free will; an environment that includes the audacity of one to question God. It requires all the power and creativity of an omnipotent, loving God and the difficult patience of a stoic detachment.

Despite the absolute wonder and perfection of such a creation, the beneficiaries thereof are hard pressed to appreciate it. Sure, there are clues. Surely God calls to us quietly, but the unveiling of the inconceivable masterpiece of creation doesn't quite bring the admiration or appreciation expected from those to whom it is freely given: Beneficiaries who wouldn't exist without it.

Well, exist they do, and what glorious opportunities they have been afforded. Conceptually, every individual is given a clean slate and an open road to selfhood. As one grows and matures to independence, unless impeded by fate or repressed by hostile environment, the opportunities to choose the direction of one's life and one's being are endless.

Though desired for all, this opportunity is taken from some. The price paid for free will, an indifferent world, will inexorably curtail the opportunities of many. The rest of us, fortunate and unscathed for most of our lives, are seated at the table of plenty.

God's gifts have been piled up high around us as far as we can see. We haven't earned them. There is no justice in it. They are loving gifts to which we are no more entitled than the unfortunate are to their troubles. But the gifts are there, and our lives are shaped by our responses to them.

The gifts are the choices inherent in this world. What we will decide to do with them will shape our lives and souls and define who we are. If we choose to be artists, then abbondanza means we have a limitless array of colors and brushes to paint our own self-portraits.

We can choose to explore any discipline, any trade, any hobby, any philosophy, any partner, any pet, any place to live, any righteous act, and any sinful act. We can choose one thing today and another tomorrow. We can even choose to increase our knowledge in the hopes of making better choices.

All of this glittering gold before us dazzles our eyes. Lifetimes could well be spent pursuing any one of countless numbers of interests. Perhaps we may choose to follow the roads to which we are best suited, but even if we didn't, our lives could still be fulfilling and self-defining.

Moreover, whatever direction, career, or life's work one might choose, it would be difficult to exhaust all it had to offer in one lifetime. The role of a parent, for example, is a role for a lifetime. It changes over time and is always evolving. An architect may be good at what she does, but there are always new challenges, new designs, and new methods of construction. The fields of medicine, psychology, law, astronomy, communication, engineering, physics, technology, and so many other professions and trades have exactly the same characteristics.

Many may become expert in their fields, but that usually requires a narrowing of their scope. A botanist may know flowers, but he may know the orchid best of all. Though it is not impossible to become an expert on a limited range of topics, it is quite difficult to do so. This is a corollary of the *abbondanza* principle. This universe not only offers a vast array of interests, but most of them are rich in complexity. One can pursue the nuances of any subject over most of a lifetime without mastering it completely. These interests will stimulate and challenge the individual to the very end.

More often than not, one's contributions to a subject simply opens the door to whole new vistas. For all his brilliance, Newton was not the end of science and mathematics, but only the beginning. Edison was not the last of the great inventors, but only one in a long line of them. And so it goes, in the world of *abbondanza*, but to focus in on this further is to uncover the further fruits of this principle.

Our lives are not lived in isolation. Our choices in life are about more than satisfying our curiosities or defining our life's work. Rather, they enhance and activate who we are becoming in a myriad of ways. Pursuing any trade or profession will be an ongoing labor, rich in challenges and in rewards, not only professionally but personally.

Nearly every endeavor offers a combination of hard work, stimulation, setback, and success. More importantly, it also presents the promise of human interaction, friendship, and collegiality. Our efforts and our goals are not pursued in a vacuum.

The principles of *abbondanza* foster the exercise of free will efficiently, meaningfully and wonderfully in a world of nearly eight billion of us. *Abbondanza* is one of the twin towers of creation and has been affecting its work from the beginning of time.

There is more in this universe than any one of us can handle, and more than all of us realize. Every field has its hidden jewels, and every age seeks to discover them. To each individual, they offer the opportunity of a lifetime of challenge and self-discovery. To those who may have chosen the wrong path and find themselves at a dead end, unfulfilled and unsatisfied, there are so many other paths. There are so many ways to grow. The fact that life is difficult, that there are obstacles, should never belie the excitement in the idea that one can choose to follow any course and learn almost anything. The recognition of this idea (along with the other concepts presented in this book) will help us see God where we could never see Him before. This path of understanding, of understanding abbondanza and its implications, leads to God.

When it does, we may move beyond the sheer opportunity of choice, to the individual who recognizes the gift and its purpose, to the individual who chooses well and in ways that deeply resonate with his soul. An observation made at my local church one Sunday, illustrates the impact such a realization and such gratitude can have.

At the moment the Eucharist is consecrated into the body of Christ, the church becomes silent. No one talks. No one responds. There is no music and no movement. The priest simply raises up the circular host for all to see and then the bells ring. One day, in that moment, a little revelation occurred that allowed me to see clear through to eternity.

As the host was raised, the altar server began to ring the sanctus bells – four bronzed half-cups fastened together. While these shimmering chimes were cast out about the congregation, I heard a small boy, a toddler, just over to my left shout out, *"Mama! I hear the bells!!"*

Once again, the priest returned to his sacred duties and consecrated the wine into the blood of Christ. As he raised the cup in silence, the bells once more began to sing their steely song. *"Mama, I hear them again! I hear them again!"* was now the cry of the delighted boy.

I remembered how Chesterton supposed heaven might be like. What is it that occurs when the will quits the battle and lays down its sword offering all to God? What is it that happens when the will ceases to sort through its universe of choice and decision, discarding the useless and seeking the true and the meaningful?

What is it that happens when time ends and there is only one eternal truth to contemplate? Chesterton surmised it was akin to a child discovering a new and joyful activity. They laugh and laugh and if it stops they tell you, *"Do it Again! Do it Again!"*6

Is this the joy of heaven, to participate in the eternal goodness of God? To be so wholly consumed in the moment that it is eternal? An instant understanding that there is nothing more, nor could ever be? *"Do it Again! Do it Again!"* and on into eternity. Lost in contemplation and joy of what is forever powerful and good?

These are the choices we have. These are the moments we seek. A never-ending parade of opportunity, if only we choose to step forward. One of the most important choices that we have is with each other. Not only is all of nature assembled before us, not only is every career path or intellectual endeavor we can conceive open to us to pursue, but so are all the rest of us.

As mentioned earlier, we should each feel this world was made solely for our own individual formation; for from our own individual perspective, it was. It is the only thing that matters until we are ready to confront our God. But we must also understand that we each are tools for all others, potential experiences in the development of their characters.

This particular aspect of abbondanza often occurs to me while driving my car. I come to a busy intersection and am stopped for a red light. For a moment, the world stops, and I realize that I can drop whatever I am doing and choose to drive my car in any direction. I could pick out anyone at that intersection and seek him or her out. I could follow them home or get out of my car and strike a conversation. They are just sitting there like me, waiting for something to happen. I must admit that the idea is a little impractical, but it simply seems to be the time when it strikes me. I could apply this idea at any time or place. The truth is billions of people exist in this world today, and I can choose to try to engage any one of them, just as Dr. Collins did in Nigeria. All are gifts from God, and they can be incredible resources and opportunities in defining my life.

It never really ends. The opportunities of self-development, through career, relationship, experience, education, love, history, experimentation, reflection, friendship, communication, expression, work, laughter, understanding, and so on are extraordinary in number and character. Moreover, they all interrelate in the weave that becomes our soulful identity.

If God must let us go, then He has, at least, tempered this world with amazing grace and abundance. If free will requires separation from God, then it also requires choice and an ability to act. Creation has given us both and more.

For with *abbondanza*, not only does God set before us unimaginable bounty, but unimaginable beauty as well. He calls to us every day with the stunning outward beauty of this universe and the incomparable structure of His design. We are called, and we hear Him. We always have. For free will is only the beginning, God, the omega. What reminds me of this most, is the setting of the sun each day. Every day, it comes and makes no sound. Though we have seen it ten thousand times, it never fails to capture us again---alluring, brilliant, powerful, magnificent. Who, but God, can create like this?

Buon appetito!

Chapter Seven
WHERE TWO OR THREE ARE GATHERED IN HIS NAME

"What lies before us is nothing compared to what lies within us."
Meditations in Wall Street
Henry Stanley Haskins

The Unity of Self

The beautiful riches and abundance of this world do not compensate us for the pain and suffering caused by separation. But together, separation from God and *abbondanza*, allow the existence of free will in each of us.

If the universe, as I have proposed, is in a philosophical sense, truly self-centric, then what will each of us choose to do with it? The universe is here at our disposal in what Annie Dillard so rightly reminds us is a "scandal of particularity."[1] The purpose of creation seems to be to allow us, for a time, to be or become anything in particular. God, in His love and amazing grace, has found a way to defer to our choices. It is scandalous.

It is also quite grave. For what will we do? To whom in particular will we turn? For the great Danish philosopher, Soren Kierkegaard, the essential challenge of life is to determine *"whether you live in such a way that you are conscious of being an individual. The question is not of the inquisitive sort...No, it is the serious question, of what each man really is according to his eternal vocation, so that he himself should be conscious that he is following it; and what is even more serious, to ask it as if he were considering his life before God. This consciousness is the fundamental condition for truthfully willing only one thing. For he who is not himself a unity is never really anything wholly and decisively . . ."*[2]

In this chapter, we will broadly examine our relationship to God. Specifically, we will focus on the idea and development of prayer in a world that is supposed to be separated from God. More importantly, we will then discuss and explore the purpose and effect of prayer. As we examine this topic, we begin to realize that we are now a long way into our quest. Some basic and fundamental understanding of the source of pain and suffering has been discovered. Already high into the mountains, our journey will begin to shift to dramatically higher and more spiritual elevations.

These final four chapters will utilize this new perspective about pain and suffering to seek and develop the full implications of this viewpoint. We have assumed God's existence, giving us full license to blame Him for the cause of pain and suffering. We see now that we may have been too rash. We see now there may be an explanation that can be grasped. Is it now possible to believe He allows pain and suffering because from the depths of His love: He wishes us to exist in freedom? Is it now possible to believe that from the depths of His wisdom, He understands more than anyone that love is not possible without freedom?

If this is so, then it is at this point that it becomes personal. Having understood the logical underpinnings of our suffering, we can now afford the luxury of assessing its full spiritual dimensions. For what does it mean to us to have such freedom? This chapter is devoted to exploring the concept of the unity of self.

PART ONE

The Existence of Prayer

*"I know only enough of God to want to
worship him, by any means ready to hand."*
Holy the Firm
Annie Dillard

Before we begin our final ascent, some practical questions concerning mankind's historical belief in the existence of a personal God who can hear us requires some attention. How is it, that in a world in which separation from God is required for the existence of free will that prayer was introduced into the world? If the creation of free will demands a design that precludes the intervention of God, then how is it that we claim to know God? How do we explain the phenomenon of religion, the belief in miracles, the propensity to pray?

Is it plausible to believe that God devised a beautiful and intricate universe in furtherance of the foundation of free will, only to undermine it all with the perpetual tinkering of direct intervention? Are we to believe that He is constantly smoothing over the rougher edges of His creation in contravention of His divine and perfect plan to create an indifferent universe, the only kind of universe possible for the sustenance and maintenance of free will?

These are legitimate questions, if not particularly difficult ones. Throughout this discussion, a sense of logic has been demanded in the creation plan, in order to secure and foster our faith in a true God. For if there is no logic to our God, how could we ever find Him? Though the principles of probability and randomness found in physics may be utilized as structural components of an indifferent universe, they are incongruent with the nature of divine judgment. The Almighty One cannot be said to have created the universe on an ill-conceived whim, thereby requiring Him to incessantly correct and adjust its imperfections.

Preceding chapters have discussed the fundamental problems inherent in the creation of free will. God, the perfect Creator, has transcended these problems in the only logical way possible: The creation of an abundant universe from which He has separated Himself. Yet, the goal of creation is not fulfilled by the act of creation. The goal, as discussed in Chapter 5, is to afford each of us an opportunity, by the grace of God, to share, understand, and participate in the overwhelming joy of His presence.

Creation, for us, is the first step of the journey back to God. Creation, for God, is the setting of the stage. With the stage set, with free will in hand, the drama of each individual life begins. As we participate in this drama, the conflict of who we are as individuals is developed and explored, as Kierkegaard would say, "before God."

In fact, that is all that ever happens in this play. Actor after actor enters the stage and attempts to resolve this conflict and define his or her individuality. Each actor uses his or her talents to discover who he or she might be. The stage grows ever wider.

Eventually, some begin to wonder what it's really all about. They never really seem to be able to understand it. They begin to look around for whatever clues they can find. They begin to discover that this stage is incredibly elaborate. They haven't the slightest idea how it works or who operates its features.

This drama, for some, becomes a great mystery. They continue to act out their roles, to discover what they can through their talents and performances, but now with a wary eye on a bigger picture. Though the stage is ever revealing new sets and scenes, some of the actors are disappearing. It is certain that this drama has tragic overtones. But each day, the curtain rises, and they ponder it all again.

By now many have come to realize that this is no ordinary production. It is also a mystery about life and death. It's a mystery about the meaning and significance of each actor.

The end of the play ultimately demands a final resolution of the mystery. As the final curtain descends, the actor must choose how to make his final exit. He must determine what will be said in his final soliloquy.

In any ordinary drama, this final choice would be nothing more that thought-provoking. In the play that is one's life, the choice is strikingly existential and starkly eschatological. It has eternal consequences.

Where does the actor go for help? The beauty and ingenuity of the drama is that it is completely improvised. There are no scripted lines. There are only the clues of the set and of the other actors on the stage. Some actors are unaware of the mystery. Some downplay its integral relationship to the exercise. Others find it impenetrable, and a few ignore it altogether. But the greatest and grandest performers draw it out. They breathe it in and pursue its wonder.

Some of these actors may come eventually to look for the producer for help or guidance. Now, the producer is there, but he sits off of the stage, behind the bright lights and is therefore unperceived. He notices the quizzical looks and glances directed his way. He hears the quick, but fervent, pleas for help when the opportunity presents itself.

By and large, however, he doesn't often respond. Most of the time, he simply offers a comforting nod of the head or a knowing smile. The actor, though reassured, learns nothing and resolutely carries on.

This is, after all, an improvisation. The beauty, the charm, the creative tension, and the significance of the work come from the players and their struggles to develop and understand their characters. Too much assistance, too much guidance, too much interference with this process ameliorates the potential fullness of the performance and the development of the actor, the stated purpose of the play.

So, it is with each of us in life. God is the producer, and His work is largely done. We are the improvisation artists on the stage, wrestling with the mysteries of life. If God interferes too often, He may smother our individuality and inhibit our development.

Notice, however, that in the above example, the producer does have the option to respond. In fact, there are times when he may respond quite dramatically, if he chooses. His response, however, must always be measured by the requirements of the improvisation, by its format. He knows that any intervention with the actors will upset the creative requirements of the genre and may prevent him from discovering honest and serviceable performers.

At times, the wisdom and compassion of the producer coincide with his professional experience and overcome the logical reluctance to intercede. In these instances, the drama is necessarily affected and altered, but in most circumstances this should be an overall benefit, so long as we can trust his wisdom and experience.

Notice also that the producer does not run out onto the stage uninvited. Once the play has begun, the producer is offstage, an interested party, but not a participant. Truly gifted improvisation artists know, however, that with the exception of illegal acts, nothing is truly out of bounds. Though the producer may choose not to respond, the actor may certainly try to draw him in. He may try to engage him quietly, challenge him directly, or even invite him on the stage. Conversely, he may entreat, vociferate, clamor, or demand. All of these methods are the actor's choice to pursue. Once asked, the producer has every right to respond, and every right to decline. The actor's attempt to engage the producer may not be successfully made, but once advanced, it becomes part of the fabric of the action.

As we leave this example, we therefore see that the principle of separation from God, which is integral to the creation of free will, does not consume or constrain the principle of free will. We may freely choose to ask God to intervene. This is the source of prayer and our right as beings endowed with choice.

God has let us go, for our own good and for our own identity. He has done what is difficult, what is necessary, and what is right. Each of us, as free individuals, has the right to invite Him back into our life. We may surmise His existence from His calling card, the abundance seen everywhere around us. We may choose His intervention and His interference. We may even choose to devote ourselves entirely to what we perceive to be His will. Once we ask, it is up to Him. Now, it is His choice. Depending upon what we ask, He may or may not believe it prudent to respond directly or immediately. He must consider the parameters of the environment necessary for free will in every response He makes if He is to respect the integrity of His creation.

Along with the gift of free will, we have also been given the intellect necessary to harness it. In accordance with the principle of 'abbondanza,' each of us may choose to explore any aspect of the universe as far as our minds can take us. Some have found interest in exploring creation itself. But we have been given the gift of the entire universe, and we may explore any subject of interest to its logical conclusion, if we wish. At least, theoretically, we have the capacity to pursue any subject we can conceive and the freedom to pursue it with as much energy as we have.

This capacity has led us to question the nature of our being and the source of it, just as it has led us to the study of any other subject. From the beginning we have been aware of our innate desire to express and define ourselves, our world, and our creator. We have sought explanation and understanding in myriad sources and methods. From mythology and pantheism, to science, philosophy, and revelation, we have expressed these desires in all cultures and in all generations.

That most of the world has evolved to believe in one God is as much a matter of history as it is divine revelation. We have been searching for God as a species for a long time. When someone comes along with understanding and wisdom, we are able to grasp it and revel in its truth. Our search is, in fact, tantamount to a request for revelation. We seek the Creator, if one there be, and ask Him to respond to us. This has been an historical process. We may choose freely what, if anything, God seems to have revealed to us about Himself. This search for God, and His response, is what has been institutionalized as religion.

Understanding God and His relationship to us is not an easy task. We have many questions and misapprehensions. Over long periods of time, we have developed a variety of religious approaches to institutionalize and memorialize our beliefs and foster an ongoing relationship with God. For the individual, it is an ongoing and evolving process. For the individual, it is rarely a simple matter of direct revelation.

It is a slow and awkward dance. We have so much to learn in regard to our relationship with our Creator, and our existence seems so precarious. It can be no other way. God is constrained by His respect for our existence as free individuals. He cannot enlighten us all by instant and full divine revelation. Faith and religion have developed as the bridge in our desire to learn about our relationship to God.

Prayer is the further refinement of that understanding, and one of the essential ways that faith may be practiced. Though God whispers to us in creation, it is each of us who may call out to Him in the exercise of our free will, and in our individual pursuit of truth.

Once sought and once invited, His response and/or intervention is natural, appropriate, and in accord with the perfect plan of creation. It is a response to our choice and respects our desire to choose anything we wish, within our limited powers to act. Moreover, it is a step toward the goal of creation, eternal joy in the presence of the Almighty, made in perfect harmony with the plan of creation, to create beings of free will and intrinsic value. It also affords the hope necessary to overcome the great price of pain and suffering paid for by the very free will that makes us relevant to God.

God does not control our every move, but He may respond to every prayer. Our prayers, likewise, give Him a chance to respond to the needs and suffering inevitably and unavoidably caused by the creation of the environment necessary for us to live in freedom. Miracles are perfectly consistent with this idea. They are great articles of faith and a special subset of the concept of prayer. We will take another look at them in Chapter 10 but based on everything we have already discussed about the principles of separation from God, we would expect miracles to have three basic attributes.

First, they should typically be responsive to pleas or petitions of the faithful and not random acts of divine lightning. Second, they should be rare so as not to overwhelm with divine pyrotechnics the free will present in humanity. Third, they should be inexplicable. The source of miracles should typically be a matter of faith and unknowable, thus preserving the principal of separation to all, perhaps, but those directly involved in the miracle.

In short, because of the principles of separation, miracles must be limited. On the whole, we should find them to be inexplicable, responsive and rare. They are performed with respect and meant to encourage, but not to coerce.

An example of such a miracle was one of the many wrought by Saint Gerard Majella in the 18th century. Saint Gerard was born in Mora, Italy, sixty miles south of Naples in April 1726. He lived only to the age of 29 but was committed wholly to God during his brief life. Canonized in 1893, he was recognized by the local populace as a saint during his lifetime. He had many spiritual gifts, and he performed many miracles. In his book, St. Gerard Majella, Fr. Edward Saint-Omer relates the following story:

> "Passing through Senerchia, he found some of the inhabitants in great perplexity. They were not able to bring down from the neighboring mountain several huge chestnut trees, which they wanted to use in the creation of their parish church. Gerard, always ready to sympathize in the trouble of others, had them take him up the mountain. He found the trees to be of extraordinary size. Tying a rope to one of the largest he exclaimed: 'Creature of God, in the name of the Most Holy Trinity, I order thee to follow me.' Then, to the intense amazement

of the spectators, he alone drew it – and without effort – to the church. At the sight of this prodigy, the people courageously, recommenced their labor, and soon all the trees were brought down the mountain."[3]

The many miracles of St. Gerard were well-known during his time, but his name is not commonly recognized today. Typically, his miracles were in response to a need and completely inexplicable to the average man or woman. Though he performed many works, they were rare enough to cause complete amazement among the people of his day.

Similarly, thousands of miracles have been recognized by the Catholic Church over its two-thousand-year history. Yet, by and large, most of them have been in response to a need or a plea. They remain unexplained and are rare enough that few have ever seen one.

The cures of Lourdes, for example, remain inexplicable even as they still occur to this day. But again, their impact, as with most miracles seem well contained. It is said that 70,000 saw the dancing of the sun at Fatima. Where are the sons and daughters of Fatima today? Why have they not risen to build the New Jerusalem?

God respects our will and will not trample upon it. Our freedom has been dearly paid for in pain and suffering. Though many miracles do seem to occur, though God may respond to our petitions, we still seem to retain the power to walk easily away in disbelief or indifference.

In fact, even the Saints may not readily breach the wall of the respect and separation that God has built. Listen to St. Therese of Lisieux, regarded as one of the greatest saints of the 20th century and affectionately known as the Little Flower:

> *"If you were to judge by the poems I write you might think I have been inundated with spiritual consolation, that I am a child for whom the veil of faith is almost rent asunder. But it is not a veil. It is a wall that reaches to the very heavens, shutting out the starry skies I feel no joy, I sing only of what I wish to believe."*[4]

Even for the Saints, the wall of separation is impenetrable. The fact that miracles are few and far between, and that the vast majority of people never experience one, suggests both that God may respond to our calls and yet is reluctant to respond too often. He is less interested in the praise and glory of the world and more interested in the miracles of the heart. For the miracles of the heart are available to us all, every day.

Rare, indeed, are the miracles of the world. Physics is but physics, powerful as that might be, but only that which is within is capable of performing miracles. Miracles are always of the heart. Nearly every miracle performed by Jesus was in response to the miracle of faith that lies within. To the woman who touched the tassel on his cloak in hopes of a cure, *"Jesus turned and saw her and said, 'Courage, daughter! Your faith has restored you to health.' That very moment the woman was cured."* Mt. 9:22. Time and again, we hear the words in the gospels, *"Be on your way. Your faith has healed you."* Mk. 10:52.

Therefore, those who seek the help of God may sometimes receive it, despite the constraints an indifferent universe requires. However, those who have faith, have already received their miracle.

In his book, <u>My Life with The Saints</u>, James Martin, SJ relates the following story about his first trip to Lourdes as a chaplain for a group of 250 people sponsored by the Order of Malta, a charitable organization. While there, he saw many extraordinary sights over a week's time. They often left him with a sense of wonder. On his last night there, a dinner was held. He relates the following conversation:

> *"Over dinner, one knight tells me that the boy with scoliosis, one of the most cheerful children one could hope to meet, said that his classmates might be sad when he returned to school. 'They thought that I would be tall and that my back would be straight,' he explained. He had visited the baths just that morning, with no apparent physical change. 'But that's okay,' he said. 'I'll be tall, and my back will be straight in heaven.'"*[2]

For this boy, a miracle of faith has already occurred. Though his life may well be difficult, he has freely accepted God with his whole

123

heart. If only I were God, how glad I would be to welcome him into my kingdom. How wonderful it is to find trust and love in the universe.

So, therefore, neither the institution of religion, nor the devotion to prayer, nor the occurrence of miracles, violates the intent of God's creation or the principles of separation. They are perfectly natural byproducts of the very idea of free will that an indifferent universe, separated from God, was designed to produce.

They do not diminish the plan of creation by introducing God into the world through the back door. They have evolved in a strictly logical sense from the principles, plans, and purposes established by the act of creation. We have, therefore, met the Almighty at the front door, and we have welcomed Him in.

PART TWO

The Purpose of Prayer

"The function of prayer is not to influence God,
but rather to change the nature of the one who prays."
Soren Kierkegaard

Prayer is a function of free will. God separates Himself from us in creation. He calls to us in '*abbondanza*.' He returns to us through free will. But we must first seek Him. We must answer the knock at the door.

Like everything else we have, prayer is a gift. If we have come far enough to realize what it is, then we see that it is a gift of great magnitude. It is the gateway to eternal life.

Though the Great Giver loves us indirectly and diffusely through the immensity of creation, in a personal relationship with God, this same immense love can come bearing down upon one like a cosmic hurricane. When in your life will you be prepared to meet such a force? How is it possible to prepare?

Obviously, it isn't going to be easy. Even Chesterton tells us, *"The Christian ideal has not been tried and found wanting. It has been found difficult and left untried."*[6] But if we are to try, it must begin with prayer.

Prayer is the communication that breaks through the separation of God from the universe. It begins in wonder, worship, and acknowledgement. It must progress to self-examination, meditation, faith, and daily living. Prayer need not occur for hours and hours, but simply as an integral part of daily life. As in all things done daily, with purpose and discipline, a time shall come when prayer has one ready to confront the will of God.

As we are all created equally before God, this requires no special talent. One is not asked to become a world-class athlete or virtuoso. Genius is not required. Even a young boy with scoliosis can do it. One needs only to discover one's best and truest self before God, to love and to prepare to be loved. One needs only to accept in faith and in the practice of daily life, that by some miracle of love, God wishes to engage each of us in a personal relationship. Prayer prepares us to accept this love.

Once again let us turn to the Little Flower and listen to her describe her "Little Way" of preparation:

"Jesus deigned to teach me this mystery. He set before me the book of nature. I understood how all the flowers he has created are beautiful, how the splendor of the rose and the whiteness of the lily do not take away the perfume of the little violet or the delightful simplicity of the daisy. I understand that if all the flowers want to be roses, nature would lose her springtime beauty, and the fields would no longer be decked out with little wildflowers. And so it is in the world of souls, Jesus' garden. He willed to create great souls comparable to lilies and roses, but he has created smaller ones, and these must be content to be daisies or violets destined to give joy to God's glances when He looks down at His feet. Perfection consists in doing His will, in being what He wills us to be."[2]

Little by little, we can work our way closer to God, but the work must begin with us. Separation, the cause of pain and suffering, allows us to stand on our own and affords us the freedom to follow our individual call to truth. "*Abbondanza*" allows us to imagine, conceive, and ponder this call, to wrestle and reckon with Eternal Truth, to determine *"that which it is I am willing to die for."* Soren Kierkegaard.[8] We must discover the flower we are and choose to be that for God. The self-centric universe is now getting smaller, but the eternity beyond it looms large.

Prayer is what free will allows for those who through their unique personal experience come to find and accept the possibility of God. It allows a connection to be made without breaking down the physical requirement of separation. It allows and anticipates a response.

For most of us, prayer begins in need and in worship. We are familiar with the command *"to love the Lord, your God, with all your heart, all your mind, all your soul and all your strength."* Dt 6:5, Lk 10:27. We acknowledge the central goodness in doing so. We are also instructed to ask for whatever we need, our daily bread. We are told to ask persistently, even shamelessly for all of our needs.

In the parable immediately following the Lord's Prayer in Chapter 11 of the Gospel of Luke, Jesus tells this story:

> *"If one of you knows someone who comes to him in the middle of the night and says to him, 'Friend, lend me three loaves, for a friend of mine has come in from a journey and I have nothing to offer him; and he from inside should reply, 'Leave me alone. The door is shut now and my children and I are in bed. I cannot get up to look after your needs' – I tell you, even though he does not get up and take care of the man because of his friendship, he will do so because of his persistence, and give him as much as he needs.*
>
> *So I say to you 'Ask and you shall receive; seek and you shall find; Knock and it shall be opened to you.'"*
> Lk 11:5-9

Evidently, *'abbondanza'* is not only laid out before us, but it is accessible in prayer as well. We are invited, and strongly encouraged, to ask the Lord for all we need. And in this asking, we see the beginnings of a relationship. But there is a catch. The next chapter of Luke's Gospel explains a little more:

"The unbelievers of the world are always running after these things. Your Father knows that you need such things. Seek out instead his kingship over you and the rest will follow in turn."
Lk 12:30-31

In every relationship trust is required. As Jesus repeatedly tells us, "what is needed is trust." Lk 8:50, Mk 5:36. In prayer, trust can be built little by little, but the trust that is ultimately required from the individual is the trust that puts God first.

Prayer is meant to be the beginning of a budding relationship with God. Thus, it can no longer simply be about the self. It is not in essence a wish list designed to fulfil individual needs or desires.

God is not, after all, the servant of the individual. Rather, God desires to set us free of our worldly desires. He seeks ultimately to set us free from the heavy burden of self-centricity and choice. Through prayer, we must work our way up to the level of trust and relationship that would allow this freedom to occur.

In a world where we may choose to live without God, the daily choices we must make regarding who we shall be and what we shall do, eventually become difficult and tiresome. Thus, we are ultimately invited to set aside these worries and allow God to show us the kind of flower He wishes us to become. The question for us then is can we let God be who He wants to be – in us?

Accordingly, it is Jesus once again who tells us:

"Come to me, all you who are weary and find life burdensome. I will refresh you. Take my yoke upon your shoulders and learn from me, for I am gentle and humble of heart. Your souls will find rest, for my yoke is easy and my burden is light."
Mt. 11:28-29

By these words, Jesus is not telling us that life will be easy. The yoke he speaks of is not the yoke of the world, for the yoke of the world is never easy. He is speaking of the existential yoke of choice. God loved each individual into existence by the creation of a self-centric universe. Though it is all freely given, the burdens of freedom never end, glorious as freedom seems to be. To find the peace Jesus speaks of, we must offer up and return the very same gifts of freedom and choice back to God.

Thus, it is said that the there is only one thing greater than freedom and that is dependence on God, who died twice for freedom: In Creation and on the Cross.[2]

We have come now to a serious point. We know what it means to enjoy the world. What does it mean to enjoy a relationship with God?

Ultimately, it must mean to forego the will. For what else do we really have to offer that is of any value to Him whatsoever?Consider, once again, that creation is entirely about bringing forth the lone individual into freedom. Foregoing the will as an offering to God means that we finally stand on the same plane. Each offers the other all that there is to offer. It means letting go of all we have been given as we grow in the understanding that it does not satisfy. It means the dawn of a wisdom that the world cannot be the goal but only a tool to reach it. It means taking the great leap of faith to a destination that cannot be known. It contemplates the subordination of the will of the individual to the will of God. Prayer is the mechanism by which the individual prepares to make this commitment. Prayer is also the means to sustain it.

Foregoing the will is accomplished exactly by discovering who God intends for you to be. The act of prayer intends to discover and pursue one's truest and best self. It intends to secure the self in truth and thereby free it from all fear and anxiety. In this freedom, love flourishes. There are a select few individuals, in each one's circle of acquaintances, who exhibit a joy of living. They are joyful in their work, joyful in their homes, joyful with their friends and with most strangers. They seem more than most, to be right with the world, and there is little that gets them down. But they are not right with the world. They are right with God. They are the flowers they were chosen to be, and in God's garden, the worries of the world are set aside. All Christians, and all who aspire to God, are called to this same joy.

Prayer ultimately seeks the joy of God's glory. It is a devotion of time and talent to the Lord. It leads to relationship, dialogue, and partnership. It is an interior journey that, one day, hopes to manifest itself in the world for God. It exposes the heart, the mind, and the soul to truth, the truth of God and the truth of you.

In a self-centric universe foregoing the will is an epic commitment. It is a stone-cold assessment of the limits of life. It is the apex of freedom from which the great leap of faith must be made for an everlasting love. Frighteningly, it is a leap that must be made without looking. The wall of separation from God is extremely hard and very real. There can never be the physical proof that God exists nor that the leap of faith is eternally rewarding.

Prayer, however, does have its effects. Though prayer cannot break down the wall of separation, it can collapse the universe into a tether line from the finite to the infinite. It drags one not into heaven, but unexpectedly into the heart. It pulls one within, as one individual before the infinite God. It leads to a dynamic self-examination, in preparation for the possibility of relationship. It leads to an understanding that saying "yes" to God is not the mere utterance of a word.

The great object of prayer is to pursue and become the unique individual you were made to be, that you choose to be, before God. In prayer, one seeks to relate to God in that unique particularity that only God and each individual can share. The whole of the universe thus narrows down into the relationship between one God and one individual.

By the miracle of love, the God of the universe desires us to return to Him. The question is: Do we want what He wants? It is an amazing concept to realize that we can dialogue with God and even say "no" to Him. But it is a cause of worship that we can say "yes." However, the undeniable truth revealed in saying "yes" to God is the simultaneous recognition that we are far from ready.

Change is required. Ultimately, prayer is essentially about this change. In prayer, we invite the Lord into our hearts. We open up and stand unshielded. We seek the Master's help, and we are predisposed to accept it. The change contemplates a transformation from self-centered to God-centered, from the admiration sought in the world to the love of God who is outside of it.

Prayer is the means and method to truly see ourselves objectively and then to seek the change necessary to conform ourselves to the good. It is the time set aside to recollect our place in the universe, conscious always of God, and to discover how to exist in His presence as His sincere and devoted friend. This is prayer.

PART THREE

The Essentials of Prayer

"Face the facts of being what you are,
for that is what changes what you are."
Soren Kierkegaard

There are as many ways to pray as there are souls to pray them. There are many facets to the God of everything. In prayer we find, as we do in the words of Annie Dillard, that *"There are no events, but thoughts and the heart's hard turning, the heart's slow learning where to love and whom."*[10] An impressive treasure of prayers, devotionals, and guides are readily at hand, but what it comes down to is the tremendous responsibility of an ineffable relationship. The God of all is accessible from every point in the universe, provided we are ready to engage Him.

What follows in this section is not a specific regimen of prayer, but a brief discussion of what is generally necessary in prayer. These are concepts to move one closer to God. Each soul must find its own path, but there are touchstones of prayer to recommend.

The essence of prayer is manifested in three basic components. First, there must be an honest opening up to God. One must expose his or her soul to God with complete vulnerability and humility. By humility, assume the traditional definition, a truthful objective assessment of oneself and one's situation. In this facet of prayer, dialogue with God is prominent.

Second, in prayer, one seeks a model in action. If the dialogue exposes some weakness, as it surely will, it becomes necessary to find the model one will choose to follow as a more ideal path in life. The spirit of love is integral in seeking this model if one is truly to adopt it and live it.

Third, if one has and continues to examine his or her life, if one has found a model for living, then ultimately prayer must lead to a quiet, courageous commitment to surrender to the will of God. The design of prayer is to bring us from who we now are to the point of commitment to act and live in life for God. It is designed to bring us to that point in faith where action is sure to follow. Therefore, prayer moves us to and sustains us in a faith-filled action.

All prayer is preparation for action in life and for a greater devotion to God. It is the process by which we find the courage to serve and suffer, to let go of the heavy yoke of freedom, and to become slaves to a higher purpose. Prayer is drawn up from the depths of one's being and is directed out in the service of the will of God. It is an interior journey, which leads one to the summit of faith. The kind of faith, which, according to Kierkegaard *"is the highest passion in a human being. Many in every generation may not come that far, but none come further."*[11] When we come this far, we find ourselves in spiritual peace as the receptacle of God's love.

As we have mentioned before, spiritual peace is not earthly peace. There is work to be done. Prayer simply leads us to the path of love's labors.

In her translation of St. Teresa of Avila's The Interior Castle, Mirabai Starr describes the interior prayer life of St. Teresa as a preparation of what she calls the "onslaught" of God's love. This is well said. We know well the trials of pain and suffering on earth, but the enormous challenge of God's love can be just as difficult. We don't often think of it this way.

The power of love, present in creation, is the power of love present within you. Are you prepared to seek it, accept it, embrace it, let it grow within you? Will you choose to become sacred ground ready for the gardener to do His work? Will you let Him plant what He will and let love grow where it may? To do so, is the greatest exercise of freedom possible for the individual.

The prayer life of St. Teresa of Avila was rich and deep. One of the Doctors of the Church, she wrote extensively in 16th century

Spain about the joys, challenges, and traps of prayer. She described a progression toward God in the various stages of prayer, from simple prayer and meditation to worldly detachment, to self-abandonment, to love, to a deep understanding of self, to the supernatural realm, to union with God.

She was a mystic who experienced profound visions, ecstasies, and spiritual levitations. She utilized vivid imagery in her writings and has given us as clear a picture of intimacy with God as we have.

The beautiful introduction written by Mirabai Starr captures the essence of St. Teresa's prayer life and is worth setting forth at some length here:

> "There is a secret place. A radiant sanctuary. As real as your own kitchen. More real than that. Constructed of the purest elements.
>
> Overflowing with ten thousand beautiful things. Worlds within worlds. Forests, rivers. Velvet coverlets thrown over featherbeds, fountains bubbling beneath a canopy of stars. Bountiful forests, universal libraries...This magnificent refuge is inside you. Enter. Shatter the darkness that shrouds the doorway...Slip away. Close your eyes and follow your breath to the still place that leads to the invisible path that leads you home.
>
> Listen. Softly, the One you love is calling. Listen. At first, you will only hear traces of His voice. Love letters He drops for you in hiding places...
>
> Be brave and walk through the country of your own wild heart. Be gentle and know that you know nothing. Be mindful and remember that every moment can be a prayer...Be still. Listen. Keep walking.
>
> What a spectacular kingdom you have entered!...That is your Beloved reclining in the innermost chamber, waiting for you,...Explore. Rest if you have to, but don't go to sleep. Head straight for His arms. And when you have dismissed the serpents of vanity and greed, conquered the lizards of self-importance, and lulled the monkey mind to sleep, your steps will be lighter. When you have given up everything to make a friend a cup of

tea and tend her broken heart...your steps will be lighter. When you have grown still on purpose while everything around you is asking for your chaos, you will find the doors between every room of this interior castle thrown open, the path home to your true love unobstructed after all...Waste no time. Enter the center of your soul."[12]

Prayer begins in the hearth-fires of the soul, within you. It is a spiritual reaction to the Other, to the physicality thrust upon us by creation which is always directed to our attention from the outside. We respond to it as we encounter it.

Now we turn within. We begin to remove the clutter and the baggage that has built up over the years of neglect. We dig deep in search of those materials useful to reconstructing our truest and best selves.

a. Humility:

A premise of this book is that we cannot talk directly and physically to God and still maintain our freedom. But what if we could?

What if we could sit down with God at the dinner table and recognize that He loves us completely? What if we could see that He is our truest and best friend and that we could safely and comfortably speak to Him about anything? To imagine this is to begin to understand the virtue of humility. This imaginary conversation has already moved far beyond conferring with God from afar about our daily needs. It is already more intimate than worship.

In the intimate presence of the goodness of God, we would feel safe enough to tell Him everything that is important to us. In the powerful intimacy of this conversation, we would not lie, deflect, or dissemble, even to ourselves. We would speak freely and put it all on the table before God. In our imagination, this all seems natural and easy to do. The virtue of humility seeks to address the difficulty of achieving honest self-awareness and expression in real life.

In prayer, we eventually attempt to move beyond need and worship to encounter and dialogue. No longer should prayer be focused primarily on our needs and fears, nor in a worship that pretends to avoid the responsibility of relationship. Prayerful dialogue requires uncompromising honesty.

As God exists eternally and immutably in His goodness, the individual now requires a move towards God. An attitude of innocence, a baring of the soul, a complete vulnerability, and openness are all necessary. One must begin, before God, to understand himself. One must begin to deeply assess his or her life. This is not simply an acknowledgment of sin, which is nothing more than the simple needs we are trying to move past.

One must examine his whole life and being to begin to understand who he really is. Only in this way can a sincere dialogue occur with the God who is not sitting at the dinner table. As discussed in Chapter 5, the Almighty has already accepted us. He waits patiently for the faith and sincerity within us to call out to Him.

Even before the birth of Christ, the Greeks knew "the unexamined life is not worth living." This most fundamental of concepts was ascribed to Socrates by his student Plato.[13] In some fashion, all of western civilization is built on this idea. It is a great foundation in the secular world of science and philosophy, but it is taken to another level in the prism of Christianity. And once again, it is Kierkegaard who describes it,

> "...really and truly a man should fear God. This fear is known to the man who is himself conscious of being an individual, and thereby is conscious of his eternal responsibility before God... talk will not go into this further. It will only ask you again and again, do you live so that you are conscious of being an individual and thereby that you are conscious of your eternal responsibility before God? Do you live in such a way that this consciousness is able to secure the time and quiet and liberty of action to penetrate every relation of your life? This does not demand that you withdraw from life, from an honorable calling, from a happy domestic life. On the contrary, it is precisely that

consciousness which will sustain and clarify and illuminate what you are to do in the relations of life...hence the consciousness before God of one's eternal responsibility to be an individual is that one thing necessary."[14]

The evolution of western thought and discovery over the centuries is a fascinating topic that is well beyond our scope here, but the thread pulled by Socrates still unwinds today. "Know thyself." This singular thread can be followed in and out of philosophy, theology, sociology, and nearly all other disciplines. It is cast in different textures and hues as it passes through the discoveries of science and psychology, but it spools out unbroken and woven into everything. From the mere pursuit of wisdom in Socrates, to the pursuit of the eternal in Kierkegaard, the central relevance of this task is preeminent for the individual seeking meaning.

In our times the 20th Century Italian Saint, Padre Pio, was renowned for his spiritual gifts. He provided the following analogy regarding the pursuit of an eternal relationship with God:

> *"He who never meditates, is like a person who never looks in the mirror; therefore, not knowing that he is untidy, he goes out looking disorderly. The person who meditates and directs his thoughts to God, who is the mirror of his soul, tries to know his faults, attempts to correct them, moderates his impulses, and puts his conscience in order."*[15]

Once we move from need and worship to encounter the Lord in relationship, then we are looking into the "mirror of the soul." We have now entered a deeper form of prayer. Here, our spiritual needs become known to us and surpass the fog of our mere desires. Worship is more vibrantly understood. Humility is sought, and welcomed, as a virtue to help us see who we truly are, to improve our vision and help us see the path to God.

A cleansing of the self and an emptying of the soul can begin. A certain detachment from the world found in and through faith can be entertained. When we take the time to see what we are called to be, we are already taking steps in our hearts and minds to figure out how to get there.

Humility is the virtue for this task. C.S. Lewis tells us that it is a cheerful virtue once we get over the initial shock of it. He believed that it would allow us to see *"that we are, at present, creatures whose character must be, in some respects, a horror to God as it is when we really see it a horror to ourselves."* He continues this thought on human character as follows:

> *"This I believe to be a fact: and I notice that the holier a man is, the more fully he is aware of that fact. Perhaps you have imagined that this humility in saints is a pious illusion at which God smiles. This is a most dangerous error. It is theoretically dangerous because it makes you identify a virtue (i.e., perfection) with an illusion (i.e., imperfection) which must be nonsense. It is practically dangerous because it encourages a man to mistake his first insights into his own corruption for the first beginnings of a halo around his own silly head. No, depend on it: when the saints say that they – even they – are vile, they are recording truth with scientific accuracy."*[16]

Therefore, when the saints look in the "mirror of the soul," they sometimes see the shocking truth of what they are in comparison to God. They see it so clearly; they understand that they cannot transform themselves into what they see. Rather they let go of what they are and begin to give it up to God. In human futility and in hopeful humility, they leave it up to God to transform them into whatever He wishes.

Humility is as bold and courageous as Joan of Arc and as humble and unassuming as St. Francis of Assisi. It is also as accessible to the great saints as it is to each of us who prayerfully choose to seek the friendship of God. Look at yourself over and over in the harsh light of truth. Forsake all pretense and do it in the presence of God. It is not a false virtue. Often confused with a meek and humble approach to life, humility is often exactly the opposite. It is the virtue of hard truth and the courage to pursue it. At its core is the nascence of wisdom in the individual. We are insignificant creatures blessed with the opportunity to love the infinite and eternal God in a uniquely personal way. In prayer and meditation, this thread of truth must always be present.

To follow this thread and allow it to weave itself into the fabric of the soul, is the journey of humility. It is not defined by turning the other cheek or by overturning the money-changers' tables, but it encompasses both. Humility is the hammer that seeks to forge the steel. It exposes weakness and demands accountability. Humility is nothing less than honesty before God in thought and in action. It is a broader and stronger virtue than we realize. And so, for example, if one of us were to say, "I am the Son of God," he would lack all humility and all honesty. He would possess an ego so extraordinarily large that the authorities would be forced to consider him psychologically disturbed. But if only I were the Son of God, it would be in all humility that I must say that I am, even if I were to be crucified for it.

In prayer and meditation, one can contemplate the wonders of the waves and the wind, the man and the woman, the infant and the infinite. One can wonder about anything and everything in the self-centric universe designed for the one who wonders, before God. And the question becomes, what does it mean for me? This is the journey of life, the epic sojourn that requires integrity above all else. It requires an honest assessment of how to become the actor that God, the great Producer, wishes one to be.

If we can honestly assess this and prayerfully, even painfully, reach a level of personal truth and understanding before God, then we have built a foundation and sanctuary which will withstand the trials of life. This truth of who we are before God, and what we can offer in return for all that He has given us, is different for each of us. But to search for this truth is to partake in the virtue of humility.

It is the greatest tool we have to build a rock of trust and faith in dialogue with the Almighty. In it, we find the reckless courage to pursue and proclaim the truths we discover. We find the wisdom necessary to accept and modify our shortcomings. We find the reason for the obedience necessary to accept the will of God. It allows us to discover who we really are and can be before God. When we do so, the dialogue that we seek has far fewer obstacles. It is then, as depicted in the great work of Michelangelo at the Sistine Chapel, that we can in all sincerity dare to extend our reach to the uncreated hand eternally extended out to us.

b. A Model in Action:

As mentioned earlier, this iconic work of Michelangelo is a work of great genius both artistically and conceptually. For me, the small space between the fingers of God and the fingers of Adam represents the entire universe. It is the concept of separation set forth in one brilliant image. This small space contains all that there is between us and God. It is a physical divide of immense proportions.

If, in our humility, we have the confidence to reach out to God, what will be our bridge across the great divide? If we have made a sincere and honest effort to assess ourselves before the God of the universe, then we realize that we may fall short of what we could hope to be on our own. As we do in many areas of life, we look to our more knowledgeable masters for advice, or we look to them as an example of what we wish to be.

If we do so in education, in occupation, in family life, why would we not do so in vocation and spiritual life? Humility reveals that there are those who seem to live better than we do, at least in some aspects of their beings. Whether a relative, a friend, a co-worker, teacher, or a religious leader, there are others who can be examined and followed as guides or mentors. Some of their traits, attitudes, and behaviors are desirable enough to be emulated.

Similarly, our guide may be one of the saints. or some saintly individual we may have known who has gone before us. Perhaps we believe that they have already crossed that great divide. A human model of life that is in some respects a reference point is an essential element of prayer.

We have said before that life is an individual journey, a Journey of One. No one else can do it for you. No one else gets to live your life. No one understood this better than our friend, Kierkegaard:

138

"The Christian heroism…is to venture wholly to be oneself, as an individual man, this definite individual man, alone before the face of God, alone in this tremendous responsibility."[17]

But there is guidance. Look around you. There are many good men and women in the world. Observe who it is that lives honorably and well. Find the Christian hero and join them in their pursuit of a soul who is pleasing to God.

We must strive to know ourselves in order to reach our highest potential. Nothing we can do exceeds the importance of the interior journey as a foundation for all that is good. To the extent that we can and do confront the essential reality of ourselves as individuals, we can discover and improve upon our weaknesses. We can accept our limitations and more generously accept the joy of the talents of others.

By acknowledging who we are in weakness, we can appreciate the need we have for the love and mercy of the Creator. What we will discover, what we must discover, is that we can assess not only ourselves, but our humanity. We will begin to discern the highest levels of human nature. We shall come to realize that when we look into the mirror of the soul we see not only God, but we see Christ.

We see Christ in human form as our ultimate model and greatest self. He becomes our guide to love and life, the greatest jewel of the human race. He is a model for us, not only in the character of His being, but in the conduct of His life. He is a model for us in His values, in His methods, and in His accomplishments, all in one life, all in one effort.

In prayer, one attempts to connect with the deepest part of the self, to break through the fears of selfishness and to bring forth a better self. One begins to determine who one is and who one should be. The model is Christ. He makes it easy for us. He not only lived a life to be emulated, but He continues to mentor us even now. His teachings are direct, simple and explicit:

"Love one another as I have loved you."
"Love your neighbor as yourself."
"Forgive seventy times seven."

"It is mercy I desire and not sacrifice."
"Fear is useless what is needed is trust."
"You will receive all that you pray for provided you have faith."
"There is no greater love than this, to lay down one's life for a friend."

Jesus showed us how, and He tells us how. Both His life and His words are more memorable and more celebrated than any other figure in human history. Of Socrates, extraordinarily little comes readily to mind, though he was a wise man. The same can be said of every other philosopher who ever lived. Of Jesus, everything is remembered, probed, studied, reviewed, and examined. His life and words have withstood the scrutiny of 2000 years. He is followed still, and by more people on the earth than of any other philosophy or religion.

If one of the models we have chosen for ourselves in life happens to be one of the saints, then He is the model for all of the saints. Prayer isn't about changing the world. It's about changing you. When Christ is your model, perfection is your guide, and love is in your soul.

The immensity of creation, the improbability of existence, the seriousness of consciousness: All call the individual outside of himself to consider his position and place in the universe. The environment is indifference and separation, the experiment is free will and choice, but the goal is love.

One may choose the love of God, the love of Jesus, or that same love as found in all the saints. It is the very same love found in the physical, which is ready to rise and expand into the spiritual. It is well within our grasp.

When you stare into the eyes of the one you love, and you see the same love returned to you in tears of joy, when the silence between you confirms all that you are, only then do you begin to realize that this, too, is from God. The great beauty in the land, the colors of the sky, the stars at night, yet, too, the laughter and the love of another, it is all part of the opportunity given and calling you home. It presents itself in the silence of the deep emotion of recognition and engaged contemplation. It is the silence of awe and reverence. The same awe we feel in love, is available in prayer, other directed and fulfilling, a great tide of emotion. Open yourself to this. Find your model. Be worthy of the joy you seek.

c. Courageous Commitment:

The last element of prayer is the courageous commitment to surrender to the will of God. If, in humility, one understands oneself; if, in truth, one has found a model of life that leads to God; then, all that is left is a commitment to act. The final search in prayer is the search for courage.

It takes the courage of detachment, and the dedication of humility, to prepare the sacred ground of the soul. When self-knowledge and the love of God begin to enrich the soil, then a spirit of detachment from the physical world can moisten it, baptize it into holy ground. Just as God created us through separation from the divine, we return to Him by detachment from the mundane.

Though accessible to all, it is not an easy road. It is difficult to find the courage, even in a spiritual sense, to leave behind all that you have and know in the world. Few choose it. Once again, one who did was Teresa of Avila. She dedicated her life to the Carmelites and monastic living. As a result of her deep prayer life, she heard the call to reform her Order and open up many new convents and monasteries all throughout Spain. It was a grueling task and not without significant controversy. Though she had many reservations, she kept to her task and continued a constant dialogue with God, the love of her life. One day, the story goes, she struggled to reach her destination on the rugged mountain roads. Mirabai Starr relates the rest of the story:

> Teresa and her nuns were attempting to cross a raging river with their donkey cart when a cable broke and washed away all their supplies. Exasperated, Teresa withdrew to meditate under a tree.
>
> There, she heard the voice of God reassuring her that this hardship was a sign of his loving friendship. 'Well, no wonder you have so few friends, then!' Teresa grumbled in reply."[18]

It is not easy. Though free will is the purpose of creation, and explains fully the presence of pain and suffering, it is not the end of the story. Choices must be made to fulfill the purpose. Perseverance is required. The story of Saint Teresa is the story of choosing to let go of the world and to hold onto God. To fulfill the purpose of creation, a certain detachment from the world, and thus from one's desires and one's will is necessary to prepare the return to God. If, as we have assumed, God exists, then the highest purpose of free will is revealed in stories and lives just like these. Choosing freely to enter into a relationship with God is the great purpose and hope of the gift of free will.

This cannot be accomplished, but through the assistance of prayer. With the sacred ground prepared and the choice made, we need only wait for God to plant his seeds. What will grow in our garden? More and more, this will be God's choice, if we continue to choose this path. Saint Teresa did. If only I were God, I would love her with all my heart.

> *"What I really need is to get clear about what I must do, not what I must know, except in so far as knowledge must precede every act. What matters is to find a purpose, to see what it really is that God wills I should do; the crucial thing is to find a truth which is truth for me, to find the idea for which I am willing to live and die."*
> *Soren Kierkegaard[12]*

Through creation, through evolution, through one's birth and formation, to this point of choosing and living for God, life on this self-centric universe has relevance to the divine only in preparation for the courage now sought. Through prayer, self-detachment and humility, the choice requires recommitment every day, and especially in the long and trying days and the "dark nights." It is difficult, as the saints well know, as anything worth having always is. Yet, Genesis reassures us that "It is good," and Jesus tells us, "Do not be afraid!"

Prayer is not simply a journey of self-knowledge, but of faith, love, and courage, of knowing oneself before God and making the leap of faith into the bonds of eternal love.

Chapter Eight
FOR WHOM THE BELL TOLLS

In our sleep, pain which cannot forget
falls drop by drop upon the heart
until, in our own despair, against our will,
comes wisdom through the awful grace of God.
Aeschylus

The Unity of Man

We walk on hallowed ground. A wizened WWII veteran, now in his nineties, was visiting one of the many cemeteries constructed in foreign countries to honor US military veterans and other soldiers. As he sat there and surveyed the grounds, he made a comment that he was well-qualified to make: *"It takes a great sacrifice to be worthy of freedom."*[1]

We have come far enough to begin to realize what this means. We have explored Genesis and contemplated our vulnerability. We have explored our relationship with God and looked again at the marvel of creation. We have examined the power of prayer and its relationship to free will. The puzzle pieces are now in place. The final realization is now upon us.

God is logically limited in creating beings of free will. To be among us and present in our world, He would necessarily overwhelm us. Our will would evaporate. It would be eviscerated, frozen in awesome contemplation of a Supreme Being. Like a candle in the sun, it would be nowhere to be found. We would cease to have meaningful existence as independent individuals of substance.

Of necessity, therefore, God has created a beautiful, complex, fascinating, but utterly indifferent world, subject to natural law and overtly logical and scientific principles, but not overtly controlled by Him. He has stepped away and offered us our will. The conditions for free will are present on earth, just as are the conditions for life.

God created both possibilities by creating the universe and then stepping away.

In some sense, this is why He rested on the seventh day. For in large part, He was done. There was nothing more for Him to do. From the standpoint of creation, and the imminence of Humanity, He has been at rest ever since. And when He rested, our time began. Time itself began.

Nowhere does it report what He did on the eighth day or the ninth day or any other numbered day. His work was done. The foundation was set. If God is to be true to His creation of free will, His active "numbered" days are over. He must leave those days to us. He can love us, hope for us, engage us, call to us, guide us in some quiet ways, but He cannot control, prevail upon, or subject us if He values the free will He created for us.

It finally makes perfect, logical sense then, that God is not with us in any physical or interactive manner. There can be no such nexus in our world. Thus, we are no longer, nor ever were, in Paradise. We would cease to exist as individuals. We would all be exactly the same in substance. We can only exist as true individual beings of understanding and significance in our own indifferent world, not controlled and orchestrated by God. As God steps away, we are possible. But the unfortunate reality is that tragedy can then occur. The world is indifferent to us. It doesn't care. Unknowingly it nourishes us, shelters us, beguiles us, challenges us, and kills us.

From the beginning, God understood the inevitability of tragedy in our lives. He feels our pain, as any Father of any child would. He feels it over and over every day. Yet even so, He made the choice to bring us to life. It is clear to Him that our lives of individuality and free will have value far greater than the tragedies we may endure.

Now, it is our turn to understand. The tragedies of this world indelibly belong to each of us. They are intrinsically related to who we are as individuals. They are the blankets of our birth. The pain and suffering, we each endure, may dramatically shape and mold our personalities, perspectives, and the very core of our being in essential, psychosomatic ways. In many cases, one may even be altered by a relationship to others who suffer pain. In other cases, this may be due simply to one's compassion and empathy for victims unknown.

The inescapable reality is that pain, suffering, and tragedy are the price humanity pays for free will. It is the price exacted by the environment that produces free will and the growth and formation of substantive individuals. If God were to prevent our misfortunes and shield us from our wounds, we would slowly begin to lose our will. All of our needs being provided, we would eventually all be the same in our perspectives. There would not be a significant difference among us. There would be no need for creativity, for skill, for social interaction. There would be no decisions to be made.

To those who have suffered and to those who will, it is helpful to know why. It seems random and undeserved, and almost always it is. As Jesus told us, it was not the sins of the blind that caused their blindness…Yet the suffering remains, and the tragedies go on.

The truth is that the suffering, borne by the sufferer, is central to the concept of physical separation from God, the essential requirement of free will. Suffering brings freedom to all humanity and the opportunity to relate back to God, not necessarily because of the suffering, but by the exercise of that free will in choosing Him. Without suffering, humanity would not exist.

It is an awful price, made worse by its inexplicable selectivity, and worse yet by our failure to understand it. We have tortured ourselves, through the ages, by wrongly surmising its root causes. Even when well understood in theory, it is all but welcome in practice.

Wisdom, however, can help us to accept what must be. It also allows for a certain nobility of character. Like it or not, the sufferer bears the burden and pays the price. When one understands the true value of this burden, one can choose to bear it with supreme nobility. Much like soldiers on the front lines, fully exposed and charging the entrenched enemy, the sufferers are fighting for a cause existentially critical for all of us. To know this is to be able to choose to accept it heroically. These are the poor in spirit. They are the soldiers of the Army of God, and their suffering sustains us all.

The best recent example I can give of this is the example of Pope John Paul II in his acceptance of disease, old wounds, and the shadow of death. In his last years, it was his constant and prolonged struggle to carry on in spite of these. Though once a strong, vigorous, and charismatic man, he did not complain to God or hide from the world. He displayed his suffering in recognition of its supreme value to life. He accepted it as a natural and necessary part of life, intrinsic to humanity, and deserving of dignity and admiration.

To understand this fully is to understand the awful truth of tragedy. Not only is it a great burden for those who suffer, but it must be understood as equally great for those who do not. When we hear of tragedies in the neighborhood or read about them as they occur throughout the world, or remember the great tragic events of history, we must eventually come to the awful realization that these others have paid, and are still paying, the price of our freedom, our free will.

Those who die at the cruel hands of an indifferent world or who suffer any of the atrocities of life, suffer them in the crucible of the decision by God to pay the price demanded by logical necessity for the creation of every individual of free will on earth.

When a child starves to death in Ethiopia, when a father witnesses the fiery deaths of two daughters after celebrating the birth of newborn twins, when 275,000 perish in the surge of a tsunami in the Bay of Bengal, when earthquakes occur in Iran and hurricanes in New Orleans, when a school bus drags a 3-year-old to death by his mitten strap, we must recognize the price they are paying.

These events and all others like them are part of each of us. They are the currency of our being. The choices made by each of us every day are paid for in the unspeakable sorrow of a billion lost souls. They are paid for by all of those who suffer loss on any given day or any given place in the world. And so, we are all connected. And every day the price is paid.

We literally suffer for one another, and we don't even realize it. It is important to realize who we are, where we come from, and on whose shoulders we stand. Our suffering is an enabler of free will. Our free will is our dearest, most precious asset. It has been dearly paid for, yet freely given to us. Each of us may someday be called upon, by fate in practice and by God in design, to pay our dues. "You know not the day nor the hour," Jesus tells us. The choices we make every moment beg to reflect an understanding of this.

For the sake of sorrowful souls and innocent lives, for the sake of a God who understands our pain and suffers for it, we must consider our status as free beings. We must soberly consider our choices in everyday life, consistent with their ability to honor the pain of our brothers and sisters and our God.

When we decide to disrespect our bodies and shorten our lives, or when we decide to take advantage of others due to the authority of our positions, or when we decide to carelessly risk the lives of others, or when we fail to carefully and honestly consider the consequences of our actions, policies, and beliefs, or when we decide to perform any petty, scornful, or dishonest act, or when we give in to laziness, apathy, or despair...are these decisions that can be justified in the face of the horrendous sacrifice of the innocents?

Righteous living is not simply obedience, but love and respect for those who afford us meaningful life from death, sorrow, and tragedy. The tragedy they suffer is a clarion call to life for each of us.

Our free will cannot exist outside our indifferent environment. The vicissitudes of tragedy randomly seek their victims. The rest of us, safe for the moment and perhaps quite unsuspecting of the vortex we navigate, carry on under the blessed banner of free will. The angel of death and destruction having passed us over, we would be wise to consider our predicament.

'and so, when in distant lands we hear the dirge and feel the hopeless shadow in a forlorn face and hear the melancholy hand of fate knocking on death's door, ask not for whom the bell tolls--It tolls for thee.'[2]

Chapter Nine
SUFFERING SERVANTS

Consider the shortness of time,
the length of eternity and how everything
here below comes to an end and passes by.
Of what use is it to lean upon that which
cannot give support?
Saint Gerard Majella

The Unity of Suffering

The bell tolls for thee. It tolls loud and strong. If you can hear it, then you hear it striking 11. For now, you are in the 11th hour. The time for action, and for doing, and for commitment is upon you. It will not wait.

For a God who loves us enough to create us and loves us enough to allow pain and suffering as an unavoidable necessity; for a God who loves and cannot take away our pain without diminishing our freedom; what else can we imagine asking? What else is there left for Him to do but to participate in it with us? And so, He does, openly, publicly, raised up into the air for all the world to see, brutally, cruelly, inhumanely by the practiced torture of Roman conquerors.

So as not to overwhelm our freedoms, he came quietly and humbly. Born into the straw poverty of an era without any modern conveniences, He came to participate in our condition at its most basic level. He participated freely, willingly, and lovingly, in solidarity with us all and with the many millions who cannot otherwise comprehend what it all means.

There are times when words and wisdom are useless. When only acts of love, compassion or heroism can communicate the shared humanity of the moment. For a God who created us in separation, yet loves us unconditionally, we can see in hindsight what was in foresight utterly inconceivable. The God of love, who cannot remove our pain, chooses to suffer with us. In so doing, He shares with us and we with

Him, the bonds of humanity in every tragedy. He stands ready to comfort us as one who has been there before us. He does so not in words, but in solidarity. He is there with us in our tears, in our pain, in our suffering, and in our grief.

In the early morning hours of April 23, 2010, a young woman and her friend were out celebrating in Chicago. Natasha McShane was a 23-year-old from Silverbridge in Northern Ireland. In January, she had come to Chicago to pursue her master's degree in urban studies.

Five-foot-tall and full of life, she came to spread her wings and explore the world. She worked part-time as a waitress as she completed her studies. She received word that she was accepted for an internship allowing her to continue her stay in Chicago. Her good friend, Stacy, had also received some good news and so they were in a mood to celebrate. They went out to dinner and stayed out to dance and party. They were enjoying life and feeling good about the future.[1]

Evening turned into early morning, and they were walking home through a neighborhood called Bucktown. The area was not generally known to be a dangerous place, yet they were seen to be an easy mark on these city streets. With his girlfriend waiting in the car, a callous and ignorant 31-year-old approached the two women from behind. He slammed a baseball bat into the back of their heads. He robbed them and left them for dead.

Natasha McShane suffered the worst of the attack. A long way from home and family, she struggled for her life. She was in a drug-induced coma for a few weeks. Her skull was fractured, and her brain swollen. Her parents flew in to be at her side. A couple of weeks after coming out of her coma, her first words to her mother, Sheila, were "Mommy, I'm sorry." She has said little since.

At first she did seem to progress. Eventually, she went home to County Armagh, but her life is profoundly different now. A second operation to reattach her skull led to infection. Two years later, the only word she could say was "sinn," (pronounced "shin") the Irish word for "we," and no one really knows what she means by it.

Most of the time she sits quietly in a wheelchair. On a good day, she can hold her teacup. Her once-bright future appears lost. Her parents faithfully watch over her, and she is comforted by her

149

grandmother and a loving family. But it is a tragedy for all of them. Her life has been stolen by a heartless, soulless act. No words will make it right.

The God of the universe foresaw and allowed this act. He did not stop it. He did not cure her. The possibility of this tragedy is encapsulated in the greater gift of freedom and life. But the greater gift is sometimes of little consolation. The words and the wisdom of a "greater gift" are not enough.

Jesus makes almost no effort anywhere in the gospels to explain the necessity of our worldly sufferings. Yet, examples of human affliction were brought to Him daily. He doesn't explain. He cures. He loves. He forgives. He offers hope. He assures us only that it is not on account of our sins. And at the end of His ministry, He drinks the cup, and He suffers.

He is beaten, whipped, kicked, slapped, stripped, publicly humiliated, nailed to a cross, and hung up in the air on top of a hill for all the world to see. He suffers a violent and horrible death. He participates. No words are necessary. He joins us in the lowest lows a human can endure. He forgives us. He offers His spirit to God. And He dies. He is therefore with us in every tragedy, and He is one of us.

By this act, by this very public display, He extends himself to us in every difficulty. As He walked the Via Dolorosa, it was no accident that He did not walk it alone. Simon the Cyrene was plucked out of the crowd to help Jesus carry the cross. This stranger, Simon, was there with Jesus, shoulder to shoulder, in the intensity of this final, painful journey to His death. In His last steps and greatest sufferings, Jesus was partnered one-on-one with humanity.

As it was with Simon the Cyrene, we sense that Jesus may never be closer to us than in the darkest hours. It is often the case in this world that the darkest hours cannot be averted, but when we carry the cross, the suffering, beaten, and bloodied Christ walks with us.

If suffering is necessary, can a more profound response or act of solidarity be imagined? The love of a loving God is shocking. We are far from ever being able to understand or anticipate it. It was the mantra of St. Teresa of Avila never to put limits on God.

Yet the bell tolls in Silverbridge. It tolls in Newtown and in Tacloban. It tolls in Mombasa and in Damascus. The opportunity for love and for service is all around, most especially in your own neighborhood. If suffering must come, resignation and despair are not the only options.

The tolling of the bell is a call to service. It is a call to relationship with God and to love. Though we spoke at length of prayer in Chapter 7, it was only as prelude to a commitment to action in service of those whom the Lord cannot reach in this world. In prayer one prepares the heart "to manifest itself in the world for God." One prepares to hear the call and to make the great leap of faith.

If one has prepared well enough to hear the call and see the need, then the 11th hour has arrived. For now, it is the time for decision. It is time to exercise the free will and individuality that was forged in creation. It is time to decide whether one has the time and inclination for a relationship with God. For if God exists, then He is calling to you in His need.

God loves us all, but some will suffer. To respond to these is to respond to God, not as a test of our love, but as a living foundation for love and relationship with God. He cannot help them all without diminishing our freedom. But the dilemma of creation is precisely the opportunity to relate to God. Love is not simply an intellectual or emotional endeavor. It requires a concrete and continuing response in action.

The basis of a relationship with God is not simply the development or offering of one's talents. To simply give back to God the very talents He gave to the individual is inadequate. What He has given away, He does not need.

The value of the individual to God, and the basis of any relationship of love, are found in the desire to give to the other all that is needed, to share in their highest hopes. Though we can certainly utilize our many, varied talents in this effort, there is really only one way to relate and give to God what He desires and does not possess. Through the great leap of faith, one must offer up one's freedom, one's will, in service to God. Thus, the Journey of One ends diffusely in the eternal union of spirit.

God has made the universe for you and for you alone. It is a place where you have been sent to forge your own identity, reality, and way of life. The tuition has been paid by God and by all of those who suffer the random acts of misfortune.

But for the susceptibility to suffering and death, there are no strings attached. God has freely and uniquely given to each of His children this universe. We may simply and basely choose to enjoy it, without care or concern for as long as it lasts. The wonders of this universe and, indeed, this world: the friendships, the experiences of love, and the fruits of labor or luck, may all be there to enjoy without ever once acknowledging God in one's life. God will not begrudge you any of it. For as long as you live, may prosperity be yours.

For the willing and the faithful, however, for the seekers of truth and of life, God has given even more. He offers a relationship. He has set forth a creation that makes relationship possible. Beyond all we have and all we can imagine, He offers the opportunity to participate in the eternal joy of His presence, to join in divine union with Him. All to be done by our choice, with our consent and not by the sheer force of His being or His will. Thus, the bell tolls once again.

How does one give his or her will to God? Generally speaking, this offering of will comes in three forms. It is done in vocations, by living and directing one's life to God in a serious, conscious manner. It is done in service to the Other, by actively reaching out to the ones randomly beset by the indifference of the universe. It is done in suffering, by the conscious offering of one's suffering to God in faith, in love or in recognition of its unavoidable presence in creation.

Simply put, it is done by putting God first in the thoughts and actions of daily life. It is an adherence to a discipline that seeks God's way and attentively abides the gentle whispers of the One. It is a soulful effort to organize one's life into living for God.

This process is preached and promoted quite effectively by the major religions of the world. It is generally done through service to others, prayer, and worship. There is no special need to detail this beyond what is already beautifully offered and practiced in many religious communities throughout the world.

However, the understanding that we now bring to this process is more brightly illuminated. Wisdom can play a larger role. This is not to say that wisdom is more important than faith. Because of the principal of separation, faith must always supersede wisdom, not all can have intellectual understanding, but all are called to and capable of faith. Wisdom is necessary only to those who have lost faith or who may question it. It is for those who have lost hope and question God's justice and presence in the world.

Our primary focus throughout this work is to explain the existence of pain and suffering in God's creation. Only wisdom and understanding can explain this. For the faithful, it is not really a question of deep consequence. It is not that they do not care, but that they trust in God that it is right. They accept that it is beyond their comprehension and they accept that God is just.

> *Blessed are the poor in spirit, for theirs is the kingdom of heaven.*

The sublime beauty of faith is that it is readily accessible to everyone. It is as simple as saying "yes." It is as powerful as the wisdom of the ages. If wisdom enhances faith, it has done its job and can do no more. Indeed, wisdom can be a great trap if it is only seen as an end in itself.

For these very reasons, Jesus takes great pains to remind us of the necessity of humility and the faith of children. It is not that God would deny us wisdom. It is to gently remind us that intelligence does not always lead to truth. Logic, intelligence, science, and philosophy are all there for us to pursue, passionately if we wish. They all may be utilized to enhance our character and they are part of the gift of 'abbondanza.' They are some of the toys in the vast playground which help us decide who we are going to be and make us what we are. But faith, humility, and obedience are safer roads, open to all and leading in one constant direction to the source of life.

In a sense, we have now come full circle. When the apple was bitten in Eden, the knowledge of good and evil came upon us. Man was confronted forever after with choice. Life in the garden, where no meaningful choices existed, and no meaningful pursuits could be had, was over.

The apple again confronts us. We are now poised to partake in a greater understanding of our circumstances and relationship to God. The knowledge acquired in resolving the perplexities of pain and suffering on earth, demands even deeper consideration of our actions.

The realization of pain and suffering as a logical necessity to the creation of free will, along with the realization that the suffering of others connects us directly to our own free will, ought to clarify and highlight the gift that we can give back to God. The doctrine of separation is an integral part of this understanding. For the realization that others suffer for our freedom, is concomitant with the realization that God cannot always help them.

We have established that the offering of our will, in vocation, in service or in suffering, is the one gift that we can bring to God that has meaningful value. It is our primary point of reference in our ability to relate to God. It is the concept that defines our viability as 'other' in a true and dynamic relationship with the Almighty.

Despite all of our prayers and pleas, miracles are just not that common. As a component of free will, we may rightly pray for divine assistance. God, through His divine judgment, will respond to our prayers as He may choose, but He cannot respond affirmatively to every prayer and remain faithful to the divine plan of the creation of free will. To do so, would bring us back to the Garden of Eden, pre-serpentine apple, where every man is Adam, and every woman is Eve.

With the doctrine of separation, therefore, the opportunity for relationship further develops. I can only surmise that the God of love, compassion, and mercy, suffers the atrocities of life along with us in some way. In response, we may not only offer our will to God in prayer, in worship and in righteousness, but we may actively seek to ease God's burden and increase the depth of our relationship with Him by serving others and softening the hammer blows that strike our brothers and sisters all over this world.

This is exactly what Jesus tells us:

You shall love the Lord your God with your whole heart, with your whole soul, and with all your mind. This is the greatest and first commandment. The second is like it; You shall love your neighbor as yourself. On these two commandments the whole law is based, and the prophets as well.
Matthew 22:37-39

Only now we know why. It is as simple as a tragic example of two young parents out for the night celebrating a happy occasion. As fate would have it, it is their last night on earth, and they never return home. No longer can they tend to their children. Never again will they hug or comfort them. Never again will they be able to teach, clothe, or bathe them. Their spirit and love will be with them always, but their greatest wish and desire is their children will be cared for and their children will learn to take care of each other.

The same is true of Our Father. Necessarily separated from us, it is His fervent wish that we will take care of each other. It is the same wish any dying parent would have. The tragedy that removed these parents from the Earth is not God's fault, but it is our opportunity.

Each act of service, kindness, and mercy is a furtherance of our individual relationship with God and in recognition of the source of our free will, it is right that such acts be taken. Each such act is again a unique gift to God that He cannot easily secure for Himself. It is a real gift with real value and virtue. If done with faith and understanding, it continues and deepens the ongoing dialogue between us. Performed in thanksgiving and gratitude for the unencumbered circumstances of one's own free will, precarious as that may be, these acts recognize with love the price paid by God and by others for our existence in the environment of true freedom. It simultaneously honors God, and others for their suffering, in a profound manner, deeply significant to them.

There comes a time in life, however, where one may be unable to relate to God in service, when even prayer and worship may not be possible. Pain and suffering, disease and affliction exist not in the abstract but in the daily reality of life. For some, it is merely an obstacle that is eventually overcome. For many others, it is inescapable, a debilitating reality of their existence.

Upon these randomly chosen innocents is built all of our freedoms. Through them, we can serve God and attain the promise of an even greater freedom, transcendence. Yet even they can relate to God in the very suffering they endure.

The individual wracked by the misfortune of enduring and unrelenting trials still has choices that resonate with God. The one who suffers may, in faith, offer this suffering to God. The one who suffers may, in the belief that God is good, choose to endure and persevere without questioning the love of God. I can only imagine that this is profoundly moving to a God who chose to make us in freedom.

Moreover, the one who now has the wisdom to understand his misfortune and the place of suffering in this world, may also choose to endure it. Armed with this understanding, one is able to suffer as an act of love, painful offerings to the Creator who made us free. These are offerings which serve the sake of all those who are called to serve. The grace of dependence is not entirely welcomed or wanted, but it can be a transcendent gift offered to the ones that serve.

In his poignant book entitled <u>The Power of The Powerless</u>, Christopher De Vinck writes about his brother who was born with severe brain damage. The book was published in 1988, but he recently reflected about it again in an essay carried in the Chicago Tribune on June 6, 2012:

> "My older brother Oliver died 32 years ago on March 12, 1980. He was a terrible brother. We never did anything together. He never played catch with me. He never advised me about girls. He didn't help build the tree fort in the woods. He never swapped baseball cards with me or taught me how to fish. My brother did provide me with some entertaining moments. Because he was blind, I spent many days when I was a boy pretending that I, too, was blind. I'd close my eyes to see how far I could get through the house without knocking down a lamp or table.
>
> Sometimes, at least, Oliver was my Zen guru. He was so quiet. Because he had no intellect, he'd just lie in his bed like a giant doll and I'd sit by his side and complain about my poor

grades in algebra or discuss, aloud, that I liked this girl Linda, but she ignored me, and if only I had a Plymouth Roadrunner, perhaps she'd pay more attention to me.

Oliver never offered advice. So, in his silence I had to discover my own answers to my woes. Algebra wasn't really important, and Jenny, the new girl, didn't care that I drove her to the high school basketball game in my father's Ford station wagon.

See? Oliver was pretty useless when I was a boy. He couldn't even feed himself. It was my job to feed him dinner: pureed fruit, warm soup, Beech-Nut baby food from a jar. Oliver couldn't chew. He couldn't hold a utensil in his hand. I had to scoop up his dinner one spoonful at a time and touch the spoon to the tip of his lips. My brother would open his mouth, and then he'd close and swallow. I never split a hero sandwich with my brother. Boys like to do that.

I couldn't even share a drink with Oliver. He couldn't hold a glass either. At each meal I had to lift his head from the pillow with my left hand and place the rim of the glass at his lips with my right hand. After Oliver drank milk, water or juice, I never heard him burp. Brothers like to hear each other burp.

Oliver couldn't even keep himself clean. When my mother and father and sister and I gave Oliver a bath, you'd think he splash his arms up and down for fun in the water. Instead, we just slid him into the tub and he'd lie there like a large soggy pillow.

Oliver was born with severe brain damage, a puzzlement that the doctors never figured out. But it was clear that Oliver did not have the ability to learn, talk, think or communicate. He couldn't work a slingshot, or dress up like Frankenstein's monster and join me for trick-or-treating, or go sleigh riding or light firecrackers back in the woods. We couldn't be best friends. We couldn't do anything together.

What good was he?

For 32 years, I watched how gently my father shaved Oliver's stubbled face. For 32 years, I listened to my mother say how much she loved Oliver as she combed his hair.

A boy mimics his father and listens to his mother. The great Russian novelist Fyodor Dostoevsky wrote in his famous book "The Brothers Karamazov," "What is hell? I maintain that it is the suffering of being unable to love."

My father taught me how to love Oliver in the way he slowly pulled down the sharp razor against Oliver's tender skin. Every morning for 32 years, my mother slowly lifted the white shade covering the window that was above Oliver's bed in a manner that was nearly religious as she let in the day's light to spill over my brother's crooked body.

The only thing Oliver could do was laugh. You could walk by his bedroom in the middle of the afternoon and you'd hear this husky laughter.

The humorist Garrison Keiller wrote, "The highlight of my childhood was making my brother laugh so hard that food came out of his nose." I would have liked to have been able to play that trick on my brother. But in the end, one of the highlights of my childhood was hearing my brother laugh, and then I'd laugh too.

We did do that well together."

The tree of suffering is profoundly bent with ripe fruit. In the difficult service of the suffering, the merciful are poised to encounter a profound awakening. Oliver was born in 1947. He was the second oldest of five children. In his book, De Vinck quotes from a magazine article that his mother Catherine wrote describing her experience with Oliver. The concepts of service and suffering embraced the realities of her life. She drew forth from it as deep an understanding as our humanity allows.

"It's hard to express what such a verdict means to a mother. It pierced me to my depth, ripped apart the very fabric of life when we discovered how severely different Oliver was going to be all his life. It was not something one could put aside or escape. The world appeared darkened. It was as if the whole of reality had been covered with a gray film. I didn't understand yet.

By the grace of God (and I don't use this as a figure of speech), I could accept it, in darkness and ignorance – yes, even manage a simple, immediate consent. I remember holding Oliver and saying the Lord's Prayer, over and over: "Thy will be done on earth as it is in heaven." I could not see the purpose of this trial, but I could say yes to God. I could begin to learn about trust, could begin to realize that God's ways are not our ways.

For many, many years, I was confined to the house, alone and without the support of relatives or friends...This enforced seclusion was difficult for me; I had a restless, seeking spirit.

Through Oliver, I was held still. I was forced to embrace a silence and solitude where I could "prepare the way of the Lord." Sorrow opened my heart, and I 'died'...I looked into the abyss of human sorrow and saw how dangerous and how easy it is to slide into self-pity – to weep over one's fate... It can also be a searing experience.

But if there is a silence that is opaque and a solitude that is a prison, there is a silence that is luminous and a solitude that is blessed terrain where the seeds of prayer can grow...Oliver was always a 'hopeless' case, yet he was such a precious gift for our whole family. 'God has chosen the foolish things of the world to confound the wise; and God has chosen the weak things of the world to confound the things which are mighty.'(1 Cor 1:27) This child had no <u>apparent</u> usefulness or meaning, and the 'world' would reject him as an unproductive burden. But he was a holy innocent, a child of light.

Looking at him, I saw the power of powerlessness. His total helplessness speaks to our deepest hearts, calls us not merely to pious emotions but to service. Through this child, I felt bound to Christ crucified – yes, and also to all those who suffer in the world. While caring for Oliver, I also felt that I ministered, in some mysterious way, to all my unknown brothers and sisters who were, and are, grieving and in pain throughout the world. So, through Oliver, I learned the deepest meaning of compassion.

I have made my peace with the coming of Oliver's death. I cannot see it as a tragedy. I know that the child who lived in *apparent void and darkness sees God, lives forever in health, beauty and light. Here on earth, he was loved. His presence among us was a mysterious sign of that peace that the world cannot give."*[2]

In vocation, we give our will to God and endeavor to follow His path. In service to others, we stand in His place and serve Him too, by joining Him in solving the dilemma of creation. In suffering, we can choose to accept misfortune and tragedy for the sake of freedom and the love of God. We can recognize the power in suffering to create the opportunity of transformation in the Other.

In 1947, a bell tolled in Vermont. For 32 years, a family answered the call. The light of love was brightly lit. The poor in spirit are both the foundation of our freedom and the opportunity to utilize this freedom transcendently. Though he didn't choose to do so, Oliver gave daily.

And his mother, Catherine, received:

"So, through Oliver, I learned the deepest meaning of compassion."[3]

And his brother, Christopher, received:

"We can stand before the Olivers of the world and see clearly who we are...Oliver also taught me about service, the deeper meaning of it. He taught me that we serve not only when we do things for others...He evoked the best love that was in us. He helped us to grow in the virtues of devotion, wisdom, perseverance, kindness, patience and fidelity. Without doing anything, Oliver made us all better human beings. The meek and humble of heart do us a service when they call us to respond in love."[4]

And those who suffer, suffer. But they also have much to give. Though he couldn't choose to give, Oliver gave deeply. Blessed are those who are able to choose or accept it, for the love of God is greater still.

Chapter Ten
INTO YOUR HANDS
WE COMMEND OUR SPIRIT

To fall in love with God
is the greatest of romances,
to seek Him the greatest adventure,
to find Him the greatest human achievement.
Saint Augustine

The Unity of Spirit

There is an undeniable bridge between love and suffering. It is a bridge that crosses very troubled waters. Even in its best moments, love can lead to sacrifice, heartache, and pain. It seeks joy, but often becomes attached to unworthy, unfaithful, or inconsistent objects of its affection.

For different reasons, suffering encounters the same bridge. It seeks the healing powers of love and mercy. It may not always have the strength or courage to cross the bridge, but it innately recognizes the hope of reformation and redemption the bridge represents.

One may cross over this bridge many times. The difficulties of life produce many anxieties. The tragedies produce great suffering. Through it all, we constantly endeavor to retrace our steps back over the bridge. We try to find the joy we were made for.

In truth, we are not particularly good at this. Through weakness, stubbornness, pride, or selfishness, we often make the same mistakes. We have not learned the lessons of love. We do not appreciate the freedoms which are the foundation of all love. We often forget that the joy of love is in the loving, irrespective of any return or reward. To be loved is a great blessing, but to learn to love is one of the great achievements of the human race.

If love is fortunate and wise, however, it finds a kindred spirit, a worthy and faithful lover who loves generously and unconditionally.

This is the love of transformation and union. It brings forth and sustains the best one has to offer.

Though even this love is not immune to tragedy, suffering, and fate, it can always be found. If not in the loving embrace of another soul, then always in the rising road, the path which seeks the heart of God.

Throughout this book we have seen how God, through separation, has painfully respected our freedoms. We recognize that He patiently waits for love to build on the freedoms He gave us. In the previous chapter, we discussed how, through suffering or service, we have something we can choose to give to God that has real value to Him.

In vocation, in service and in suffering, we can give back to God what He desires and hopes for. We can return, to God, the love born of being made in His image, a true love made and chosen in freedom. A love which breaks free of the self and ventures out into the universe of Other, the place where the God of joy is found waiting.

And in this place the love is real. It is not merely the love of formal worship or rote prayer, but real love which breathes fire and aims to give back to God what He dearly desires and values: Someone to cross the bridge, someone to care for the least of our brothers, and to heal the random suffering of the innocents.

This giving to God, therefore, is not a gratuitous notion imposed upon us by God or religion to remind us of our insignificance. It is not a grand design to extort obedience out of our freedoms. Rather, it is the coin of the realm in the Kingdom of God. It has currency and real value to God. It alleviates some of the suffering He could not avoid in creation. It honors our gift of life and freedom. The giving sought by God is found in acts of mercy and love. Remember the words of Jesus, *"It is mercy I desire and not sacrifice,"* Mt. 9:13, for it is mercy that leads to love.

When one person gives to another, what the other dearly needs and desires, then the basis of love exists. If it is mutual and accepted in action, then true love arises, and a joining of life can begin.

When an individual finds love on earth, he begins to enjoy things he never did before. He loves to see the world through his partner's eyes. A new appreciation for country music or jazz may develop.

Perhaps, he begins to frequent Thai restaurants or learn more about modern art. Perhaps, he begins to read more, dress differently, or adopt different figures of speech. A lover always notices the way his partner reacts to the little happenings in life. In this love, change occurs. This change is the point of fascination in all love stories. The change and evolution of the heart is the singular attraction and the mesmerizing force in the telling of these tales.

Imagine, then, how it is when you love the Lord and see the world through your lover's eyes. A radical change of perspective is experienced. Now, you have risen to a wholly different quality of being. Your hold on the world is diminished. Your tight and dependent grip on the world's ways is relaxed. No longer immersed in the world, or the self, you become lost to love and detached, a wholly new being, reborn to life, alive in love, generous and compassionate. Such a love leads one to endeavor to live in the present, to live in each moment with the Lord, to create in each moment a gift of being.

Over time this is no longer a physical encounter, but a spiritual one. As it was for Avila and all of the saints, the physical becomes primarily a conduit to the spiritual, a pipeline to the eternal. One learns now to express spirituality through the physical. One is given over to what is seen through her lover's eyes. *"It is mercy I desire and not sacrifice,"* Mt. 12:7. We are called to love and to serve. We are transformed and sealed in a new dimension.

God does not need our love, but He does desire it. He affords us the opportunity to know Him, however imperfectly, and to love Him, however imperfectly. When we are in love, we seek our lover. We do not hide or avoid or run away. We go to where He is. We find Him where the poor are, and we love Him there. We hear Him speaking to St. Peter: *"'Simon, son of John, do you love me more than these?' 'Yes, Lord,' he said, 'you know that I love you.' At which Jesus said, 'Feed my lambs.'"* (John 21:15), and we become shepherds too.

We find the radical example of Mother Teresa to be perfectly reasonable. "To a man who saw her cleaning the wounds of a leper and said, 'I wouldn't do that for a million dollars,' Mother Teresa replied, 'Neither would I. But I would gladly do it for Christ.'"[1]

We find the simple, but unexpected words of Jesus to overflow with warmth and acceptance. Describing one of her many visions of the Lord, Saint Theresa of Avila, reported that as she was ascending the convent stairs she saw a child. The child stopped her and asked her who she was. She told him that she was *"Theresa of Jesus."* The child said in response, *"I am Jesus of Theresa,"*[2] simple words profoundly expressing the unity of spirit and will sought by God, words that this Saint carried with her the rest of her life.

In this love that lovers have, they serve their lover faithfully. The story of faith is the story of a man or woman beginning the journey, beginning to let go. Each and every ordinary person is called to live a great life. Many do. Some are well known for it. Some come to be called saints. For all of these once ordinary people, their acts and lives are a function of their relationship with God. They are in love. They let go of their life. They deepen their love through prayer and communication. They serve and obey. It is never easy. Sometimes, they are rewarded in this love with great understanding and wisdom. Sometimes, they are rewarded with revelations about their lover and sometimes with the inspiration of His miraculous powers.

Of these to whom God has been revealed, nothing stops them. St. Stephen was the first martyr, stoned to death for preaching about Jesus. Ten of the first twelve apostles were martyred, as was St. Paul and as many as thirty-three of the first popes. Like St. Joan of Arc, and so many more, the knowledge of God's love given in revelation completely altered their lives. Overcome with love and the meaning of life, they did the will of God and were willing to pay any price. Blessed with the graces of revelation, they show us the way.

God has let us go first and best. He has released us into our own domain, into our own experiences, minds and spirits. If we learn how to give ourselves back to God, then we will surely share in the divine goal of creation. As God let us go, we must let go. We cannot give as much, but we can give all that we are. In so doing, we let go of ourselves, devote our activities or sufferings to God and others, and begin to approach the will of God.

When we do so, we may find that losing everything, helps us gain everything. To submit one's will totally to God, is to call forth the gift of union. Ultimately, what we see from the saints is that a unity with God is possible. God and the individual may become spiritually one.

It is said that this was the gift and blessing of St. Gerard Majella. He had the faith of a child and the fanaticism of a fool. Some called him the 'Madman of God.' Most others simply called him 'Saint.' When last we spoke of him, he was dragging a massive chestnut tree by himself as if it was a stick. He was capable of much more.

Born in the little mountain town of Muro Lucano, Italy, in 1726, he had been favored with a special spiritual connection to God from his earliest days. As reported by Father Edward Saint-Omer in his biography of the Saint, little five-year-old Gerard visited Our Lady of Graces chapel at Capotignano one day. Inside stood a statue of the Blessed Virgin holding the Infant Jesus in her arms. According to Saint-Omer,

> "scarcely had he knelt down when the little Jesus, leaving his mother's arms came to play with him and gave him a loaf of extreme whiteness. The child joyfully carried the present home to his mother. In great surprise, she asked, 'Who gave it to you?' 'It was a beautiful lady's child with whom I have been playing.'"[3]

Thereafter, Gerard ran daily to the chapel and each time played with the Infant Jesus and brought home a white loaf. Curiosity finally led first his sister, and then his mother, to follow him to the chapel and witness the occurrence.

Similarly, when still a child, a priest found him kneeling before an altar one day and asked him why he was there. His reply, Saint-Omer tells us, was "A little child came out of the tabernacle and gave me Holy Communion."[4]

Understandably, Gerard was passionately attracted to religious life and practices. He said the rosary daily. He went to communion, as often as he was allowed. He had an affinity for the Passion suffered by Christ, and he scourged himself as the price of his participation in every communion he received. Gerard was devoted both to the joy and the suffering he could share with his friend, Jesus.

His family worked hard to make ends meet, but tasted hardship when Gerard's father died. Gerard was twelve by this time. He apprenticed as a tailor in his father's footsteps and accepted as a gift from God cruel treatment by the tailor's foreman. Conversely, the tailor, who always thought well of Gerard, observed him in a state of prayerful ecstasy one day and ever after thought him a saint.

At the age of sixteen, he took employment in the house of the Bishop of Lacedonia. The Bishop, by all accounts, was a most difficult man. As was now his life-long habit, Gerard worked excessively hard and suffered all manner of complaints and reprimands with silence and humility. He ate extraordinarily little, usually only bread, and discovered that by using bitter herbs on his food, his appetite would lessen still.

In one famous incident, he accidentally dropped the key to the Bishop's residence down a well. Distressed at the consternation this would cause the Bishop, he began to pray. According to his biographer, the following then occurred:

> "Suddenly, filled with confidence, he ran to get a statue of the Infant Jesus, which he let down into the well saying, 'It is for Thee, Lord, to bring me the key, that the Bishop may not be put to trouble'...In the sight of a crowd of bystanders, Gerard drew up the Infant Jesus holding in His hand the lost key. This well was thenceforth called, 'Little Gerard's Well.'"[5]

The Bishop died when Gerard was eighteen, and he returned home to resume his apprenticeship as a tailor. *"With his mother's consent, he divided his earnings into three parts: one for the family, one for the poor, and the third for the souls in Purgatory."*[6]

He ate so little now, that his mother was in constant worry. *"Her friends consoled her by telling her that he was a child of Heaven."*[7] In imitation of the Lord, he practiced ongoing mortifications, He implored his friends to scourge him with wet cords, until he bled all over his body. Very often, he spent entire nights in the church in order to pray and be close to the Lord. He would attend every Mass offered each Sunday. As the ways of the world were not the ways of Gerard, he was ridiculed and derided by many of his townspeople.

At the age of twenty-two, he was rejected for the second time by one of the orders of the Church on account of his frail health. The following year, the Redemptorists were conducting a mission in Gerard's hometown of Muro Lucano. He approached them and was again dissuaded to join on account of his physical weakness. Both his mother and sisters tried to discourage him. Upon the advice of the Redemptorists, they even tried locking him in his room until the mission was over. Gerard, however, could no longer be dissuaded. He tied his bed sheets together and climbed out of his second-story bedroom window. He left them a note saying, *"I am going to become a Saint. Think no more of me."*[8]

In what must have been one of the greatest visuals in the history of Christendom: Poor, slender Gerard Majella, a gangly young man of twenty-three, could be seen running all alone down a rugged mountain road, chasing after the departed Redemptorists, chasing his dream and his destiny. He would have only six years to live.

Father Cafaro, the Superior of this Order, finally relented and sent Gerard to the convent in the town of Iliceto with the following note. *"I am sending you a useless brother."*[9] Father Cafaro was mistaken. Gerard impressed everyone with his zeal, his tireless work, his obedience, and his devotion to God. He worked as a gardener and sacristan during this time. Within three years, he was formally admitted into the Order of Redemptorists as a lay brother. By then, Father Cafaro, his spiritual advisor, had this to say, *"His whole life was a continual wonder. Our Lord had in all things raised him above his fellow men."*[10]

Though signs and wonders had always and often been attributed to Gerard to this point, in the next and final three years of his life as a lay brother, they came forth in such a fury that he is called the Wonderworker of the 18th Century. Saint-Omer recounts that he performed some miracle or supernatural sign daily from this point forward.

The immense love and devotion Gerard held for God, for Jesus, and for Mother Mary was evident to all. It was evident in his work, in his joy, in his prayer life, and in his obedience and devotion to the

Redemptorist Order. Gerard was incapable of hiding it. His greatest daily desire was to receive Holy Communion, to receive his Jesus. He was overwhelmed by the fact Jesus made himself a living prisoner, in the form of the communion host, for the faithful to receive. For this communion, Gerard prepared himself constantly in prayer, penances, service, and obedience.

So deep was his desire for the Lord, so constant his preparations, that it is said not a single hour of his life went by without thoughts of God. He was particularly devoted to the Passion of the Lord and from this his mortifications followed. He was once distressed to perceive that the Lord tried to temper his penances. His reply, *"Oh my God how canst thou address such a reproach to me? Is it not thyself who hast taught me these follies?"*[11]

With the intensity of this love, Gerard found himself frequently in ecstasy, as if transported to another world. Levitations, flights, and bilocations were also witnessed on many occasions. They were witnessed in his community and the public at large. Saint-Omer relates the following stories:

> *"One day when he had the care of the kitchen, after having received his God, he retired before a large Crucifix to make his thanksgiving. At the dinner hour, nothing had been prepared. Gerard was sought everywhere and at last they found him, entirely absorbed in God, his face inflamed. 'What have you been doing?' said a brother to him. 'There's nothing ready for dinner.' 'Man of little faith,' responded the holy Redemptorist, 'what have the Angels been doing?' The Angels had indeed been at his service, for at the usual hour a meal was served as on the best of days."*[12]

In Olivetto, while staying at the house of the archpriest Don Salvadore, the following was observed:

> *"At the dinner hour, the archpriest went himself to invite him to dinner. But to his astonishment, he found the brother ravished in ecstasy and raised about 3 feet from the ground.*

Filled with amazement he withdrew, but returning shortly after, he found him in the same state. The whole household, far from sitting down to dinner, awaited the guest with tears of emotion. 'Please do not wait for me,' said he to the archpriest. 'I do not wish to inconvenience you.' To preserve the memory of this rapture, the archpriest marked on the wall of the room the height to which he had seen the Saint elevated."[13]

This same feat repeated itself on Good Friday, 1753. When a picture of the crucified Christ was carried into the church, he was seized in ecstasy and raised before all present, totally absorbed by the image depicted. Ecstasies and transports were rather common with Gerard, as were all manner of other miracles.

In Iliceto, he restored the lungs of a consumptive. In Auletta, he cured a little girl crippled from birth. Cries of "Miracle!" spread throughout the town. In Calitri, he raised up a beast of burden from death with the Sign of the Cross, thus repaying the kindness of his hosts. In Iliceto, he cured a young man of cancer to the leg. In his hometown of Muro Lucano, he cured a young woman near death for whom the doctors had no hope.

Again, while in Muro Lucano,

"The son of Alessandro Piccolo of Muro had a severe fall. He lay on the ground without speech or motion. 'He is dying! It is all over with him,' resounded on all sides. The servant of God, touched by the affliction of Alessandro, his friend and host, approached the youth, made the Sign of the Cross on his forehead and said to him: 'It is nothing, my son, it is nothing.' At these words, the dying boy rose up perfectly well."[14]

Throughout the countryside of southern Italy, he fed the poor, cured their ills and gave them hope.

"One day going into a little cottage, he asked the poor woman who dwelt there to give him a morsel of bread. 'Alas!' she replied, 'I have nothing but a handful of meal.' 'What you have

*nothing, and this chest full of bread?' exclaimed Gerard. 'It is
empty,' replied the woman.*

*'Let us see, open it!' said Gerard. Wonderful to relate it was
full of bread.*

The poor woman could not believe her eyes."[15]

In Melfi, a widow named Victoria Bruno sold some wine, but
found it spoiled when the buyer came for it. Saint-Omer continues:

*"Gerard, happening to call that day at the house, was
informed of the loss of the wine. 'Oh, that's nothing, that's nothing!'
he said, and at the same time advised the distressed widow to
put a little picture of the Immaculate Conception into the cask,
and the wine would become good again. As Victoria hesitated to
follow the counsel, the Saint said, "Is it you who will restore to the
wine its good quality? No, it is God; therefore, do as I tell you.' The
woman obeyed and the wine at once regained its excellence."*[16]

In the farm fields on his way to Corato, he met a farmer distraught
over an infestation of mice. Without his crops, he could not support
his family. According to his biographer:

*"Gerard raised his hand, made the Sign of the Cross toward
the devastated field, and at the same instant the ground was
covered with dead and dying mice. At the sight of this prodigy,
the farmer, beside himself with joy, ran to Corato exclaiming
'The Saint is here! The Saint is here!'"*[17]

In September of 1753, Gerard was given charge of a group of
young Redemptorists making a pilgrimage to the popular grotto of
Michael the Archangel on Mount Gargano. For this trip of nine days,
he was allotted the sum of only twelve francs (about three dollars) for
the entire group of nine or ten men. As fatigue and worry mounted,
Gerard would only say *"God will provide."*

All along the way, Gerard worked one miracle after another.
To a young and healthy religious sister in Foggia, who came to him

170

for advice, he prophesied her imminent death and counseled her to prepare her soul accordingly.

By the time they reached Manfredonia, they were down to their last few cents. Gerard spent them on a small bouquet of flowers and brought them to the local church. He placed them before the tabernacle saying *"See, Lord, I have been thinking of thee. Do thou deign to think of my little family."*[18] A witness to this act invited them all to dinner. In return, Gerard cured his mother who had been ill for two months.

They ascended, by foot, to the steep heights of Mount Gargano. At the grotto of St. Michael, they prayed a long while with Gerard. As they were about to withdraw, they discovered him praying in a state of ecstasy. They prayed at the grotto the following morning as well and then retired to eat. Once again, the pilgrims faced the problem of securing a meal with little or no money. Saint-Omer describes how that problem was solved:

> *"Dinner hour having come, Gerard told his young companions to sit down at table. At this order, they regarded him with astonishment, for they thought the purse empty. 'Men of little faith,' said Gerard to them, 'sit down at table!' Then giving some money to the hermit, he requested him to go buy some bread. The latter went downstairs and returned quickly. But what did he see? A table covered with fish and Gerard distributing to everyone his share."*[19]

To a man who denied them a drink from his well, Gerard caused it to go dry saying, *"You refuse water to your neighbor whom you ought to love as yourself. Now see, the well in its turn will refuse it to you."*[20] Needless to say, Gerard and his young men were then invited to take all they needed.

They continued their journey back to the convent at Iliceto. All along the way, benefactors appeared out of nowhere. Some brought them food. Some provided them lodging. A few simply walked up and handed Gerard some money. According to Saint-Omer, they returned to Iliceto with more money and provisions than when they started.

By now, his exploits were well known throughout the region. In late November of 1753, a deadly epidemic broke out in the city of Lacedonia and the Bishop summoned Gerard. He was received as an *"Angel from Heaven:"*

> *"The entrance of the servant of God into the desolate city resembled the passage of the Saviour through the cities and towns of Judea...He was seen traversing the city, distributing to all the consolations of his charity without the distinction of persons. Some he exhorted to patience, others he disposed for death, and a great number he cured. One would have said that a celestial power radiated from him for the cure of body and soul."*[21]

In the winter of 1754 –1755, great suffering occurred in the region. The winter was severe, and many were starving. Father Cajone, the rector of the convent at Caposele called for Brother Gerard and ordered him to provide for the hungry. He provided for them places of warmth, clothing (including his own), and food. Every day they came. *"Food visibly multiplied in his hands."*[22]

To the great consternation of the baker, Gerard one day gave away all of the bread, leaving none for his fellow brothers. The baker sought out the Rector to complain:

> *"Father Cajone sent for the culprit and reproved him for his indiscreet bounty, since the late hour prevented the purchase of more bread in the city. 'Fear nothing, dear Father,' replied the friend of the poor, 'the good God will take care of us.' Then turning to the baker, he said to him: 'Dear Brother, let us go see. There may be some left.' The baker declaring there was none, opened the bread press. It was full! 'Oh,' cried Gerard, 'may God be forever blessed!' And he ran off to the church to thank Him. The other brother, truly amazed, said to Father Cajone, who now appeared, 'O dear Father, Gerard is a real Saint! I assure you there was not left a single loaf, and now we have a number of loaves. It is God who has done it!"*[23]

In Naples, Gerard wrought yet another great miracle in the summer of 1755:

> "One day, when journeying along the seashore, he saw at some distance an immense crowd who were rending the air with their cries and lamentations. A furious tempest was raging, and they were watching with fright a vessel filled with passengers and which looked as if it might at any moment be swallowed up in the foaming waves. Moved to compassion, the servant of God made the Sign of the Cross over the furious waters, threw his mantle from his shoulders, and stepping into the waves, called out to the vessel: 'In the name of the Most Holy Trinity, pause!' Then he laid hold of it and drew it in like a floating cork to the shore, he himself walking through the waters without even getting his clothes wet. 'A miracle! A miracle!' resounded on all sides. The enthusiasm was indescribable.
>
> They wanted to surround him and give him testimonies of veneration, but the humble brother fled toward the city as if he had committed some crime and took refuge in the house of a friend, which he did not leave until after dark.
>
> 'How were you able to draw the vessel?' asked Father Margotta.
>
> 'O Father,' was the answer, 'when God wills everything is possible.'
>
> Questioned later by Father Cajone with respect to the same prodigy, Gerard answered smilingly, 'I caught it with two fingers, and drew it to shore. In the state in which I then was, I could have flown in the air.'"[24]

As you can well imagine, for a man who performed miracles every day for three years, these are but a few of the signs and wonders attributed to this extraordinary saint. Among many other gifts, it is reported that he could read the state of souls and caused many to make a good confession by describing to them the sins they needed to account for. He so loved the virtue of obedience that he could hear the mental orders of his superiors though not anywhere near them, nor even in the same town.

Barely having learned to read and write, he had an infused knowledge which brought the learned to him for their own instruction. A priest from Conza, named Camillus Bozzio, happened to see Gerard in the town of Atella one day. The simple lay brother was preaching to a group of priests and laymen. Taking offense to the idea of a simple lay brother in such an elevated station, Canon Bozzio chastised him in front of everyone as an ignorant brother.[25]

This public humiliation delighted Gerard, but Canon Bozzio soon changed his mind about what he had said. He later wrote that *"Learned men are silent before this poor unlettered Brother. He draws knowledge from its source, the heart of Christ, not from the muddy cistern of the human mind. In his mouth the most obscure mysteries become luminously clear."*[26]

He could predict the future course of souls. He converted hundreds to a truer and closer relationship with God. He confronted many over their deplorable religious lives. He brought many to vocations within the church.

For himself, he had a special devotion to the needy and the ill. In the Church, he is known as the patron Saint of Expectant Mothers due to his affinity for children and their mothers. He cured many young children. While still in Muro Lucano, and before his vocation as a lay brother, he heard the cries of little Amata Giuliani while walking by her home. Upon entering, he learned that some days earlier she had fallen into a pot of boiling oil. She was burned all over her body, and no treatment would console her. Gerard held her and affected an immediate cure. By the next morning, no trace of the burns remained.

In his last weeks he had the occasion to visit a local family. As he departed the house, he left behind his handkerchief. A young girl ran out to return it to him, but he advised her to hold on to it as she would someday have need of it. Years later, and near death in childbirth, she remembered the Saint, whom she loved, and called for his handkerchief. The danger immediately passed and both mother and child were delivered healthy and well.[27]

As all who knew him came to see, the life of this man was a continual wonder. Saint Gerard died of consumption and dysentery at Materdomini in Caposele on October 15, 1755. According to Saint-Omer, he confided to Father Cajone in his last weeks that he had conformed to the will of God in everything:

> "'I look upon my bed as the will of God for me and consider that there I am nailed to the divine will. It seems to me that the will of God and I have become one and the same thing.' Later on, he caused to be placarded on the door of his cell in large characters: 'Here we do the will of God, as God wills it and as long as God wills it.'"[28]

In the years following his death, more and more miracles were attributed to his invocation. His reputation continued to grow. Saint Gerard is actively celebrated, not only in southern Italy, but also in Ireland, Belgium, and the United States. Even so, and despite his amazing life, he is not that well known even by Catholics. The principles of separation are stubborn and inescapable. Even though a wonder worker performs good and saving miracles before our eyes, he is soon forgotten. The gift of free will is buried deeply within us and not easily overwhelmed. Despite the miraculous, our freedoms remain well preserved.

To what do we attribute the miracles of Saint Gerard? There are too many stories and too many witnesses to deny them. There are too many names involved and too many places. A contemporary of Gerard's, Father Tannoia, wrote the first biography of him, called the Life of Brother Gerard. He did so after, he too, experienced a life-saving miracle by the saint. Documentation is present, from the very beginning. Moreover, the Catholic Church is well known for the exceedingly strict standards it has in declaring anything a miracle.

No, it is too easy, and too disingenuous, just to deny them. But where does this kind of power come from? It is too simple to say it comes from God. For how is it that Gerard Majella could perform so many of them, so easily, and very few in all of history have been able to perform any. It seems that Gerard himself was able to tell us by his life and by his own written documents.

His prayer life was exceedingly rich. He maintained a constant dialogue with the Lord and his entire life was in the form of a prayer. His willingness to detach himself from the physical world, raised him up spiritually. His mortifications and penances kept him physically connected to the suffering Christ, in solidarity and love. These acts all demonstrated his constant love and real-life devotion to God.

True to this love and devotion, he lived a heroically virtuous life. It is said that he was not known to have committed any sin in his life. Moreover, though blessed with revelation that to some extent impinged upon his earthly freedoms, he fully chose to have God in his life.

In St. Gerard, we see a man who chose to do the will of God in each of the three ways we have identified. He served Him in vocations as a lay brother and Redemptorist. He gave himself up to the needs of his fellow men and women. He chose to suffer. His life clearly, therefore, must have been pleasing to God.

Without in any way diminishing the above, it is the words of Gerard which may be even more telling. While a lay brother, his spiritual director ordered Gerard to give a written account of his beliefs, desires, and practices. In the simplest of ways, it offers great insight into the life of this saint and the source of his divine powers.

He was told to describe his mortifications, his desires, his sentiments, and his resolutions. For our purposes, a few revealing samples have been selected.

> "**Mortifications**: *Every day, I take the discipline, and I wear an iron chain around my loins. On retiring and again on rising, I make a cross on the floor with my tongue. I put bitter herbs in my food at dinner and supper. I chew bitter herbs three times a day. I recite six Ave Marias, morning and evening, with my face to the ground. On Wednesday, Friday, Saturday, and on all vigils I eat kneeling, and on these days, I leave untasted the fruit at table. On Friday at dinner, I eat less. On Saturday, I fast on bread and water . . .*"[29]

"**Desires**: *I desire to love my God very much, to live always united to Him, to do anything for Him, to conform in everything to His holy will, to suffer much for Him.*"[30]

"**Sentiments**: *All that we do for God is a prayer. Some occupy themselves in this, others in that; my only duty is to do the will of God. Nothing costs when we act for God...It is a very great pain to suffer and yet not to suffer for God. To endure everything is nothing when we suffer for God. I wish to act upon this earth as if there were but God and myself.*"[31]

"**Reflections**: *If I should be lost, I lose God; and God lost, what remains to me?*"[32]

"**Resolutions**: *My great resolution is to give myself entirely to God...These words: 'I will' and 'I will not' shall never cross my lips. Thy will, O my God, and not mine! To do the will of God, I must renounce my own. Yes, God alone, and if I Wish but God alone, I must renounce everything that is not God. In nothing will I seek my own interests.*"[33]

The words "'I will' and 'I will not' shall never cross my lips." From an early age, Gerard was called by God. He never wavered. He never looked back. He understood and accepted the challenge. His was a remarkable soul of courageous commitment. He walked the rising road. He loved God with his whole heart and being, and he pursued his love with passionate dedication. His whole life is a testimony that he fulfilled his calling.

How does the Greatest Giver respond to such a life? If indeed, God made the universe in freedom, for each individual soul, how does He respond to the soul of love and courage who gives it all back? In Gerard Majella, we see the answer.

Gerard's devotion was so great, it is said that his will was one with God's. It was a rare and remarkable convergence. Within it, we have a glimpse of the eternal bonds of spirit. Gerard sought, and achieved by grace, union with God. At that very point in time and space, the cosmic tables were turned, and God began to do the will of St. Gerard, for they were one and the same. Miracles poured forth with alarming ease. He could fly, bi-locate, multiply loaves, cure the sick, command the animals, the trees and the waters. His God was a willing and loving partner. He poured His Spirit into the heart of Gerard.

The Great Giver responds to all that He is given. In the life of Gerard Majella, the possibilities and power of spiritual union were revealed. In the 18th century, a comet blazed the night-time sky, and the power of God inspired the deepest hopes of the human heart.

More than anything else, the life of Saint Gerard speaks to us of divine union. It is the very hope and purpose for which He created us. It is the eternal home to which we are called.

In the beginning, the Creator chooses us. In the end, do we choose Him? All there is in the universe comes down to one choice – our response to a love proposal.

The great goal of creation is vividly expressed in St. Gerard's daily affirmation and acceptance of this proposal. His life was a testament to its possibility and to the ineffable love present in eternal union. In Gerard Magella, we see the words of Christ in full application: "He who loses his life will save it and he who saves it, loses it." It is an exceptionally fine line to walk, a thread to follow all the way through the eye of a needle and in between the fingertips of separation dividing Adam from God.

Inevitably and inexorably, the study of pain and suffering, and of the tragedy allowed to occur in this world, leads to the self. In the deepest, darkest corner of all that exists, the self stands alone. Here it confronts the ultimate dilemma. How does it extend its finite self into the infinite? The very question shapes and informs our essential humanity. For hope becomes, of necessity, the only solution of consciousness. Hope is the essence of human nature and there is but one hope – eternal life.

Thus, we are compelled to search, and the question is can we accept what we find: A love that cannot be fully comprehended, a creation that cannot be known, a presence that cannot be proved, and a love that submits itself to murder? In the search that hope inspires, can we accept the mystery and paradox of a God who loves us enough to expose us to all manner of freedom and danger? Do we find the fortitude and love necessary to let go of that freedom and choose God?

When the cause of freedom is understood, the call to return to God, to love and to divine union, then it is understood that the greatest treasure of freedom is unveiled only in its surrender.

Imagine the joy of Avila when she learned the value surrendered freedom could bring: *"I am Jesus of Teresa,"* the boy replied.

Likewise, St. Gerard found the greatest value of freedom came only from trading it in. The Little Flower reminds us that not all are called to be great saints. This great saint, however, was called to become a visual and historical embodiment of the promise of eternal union. Freedom, to him, was a curse that he fought with all of his being. He fought it with great tenacity, and he set himself on a path of fasting, penance, poverty, and prayer designed to suffocate his worldly freedom. From this great effort and desire a divine relationship of love and union evolved. Its depth and quality confirmed by the exercise of divine power, the result of a new, unified will.

In this joy of divine relationship, freedom is lost, and the exercise of individual will a great impediment. A different kind of bell is heard now. Not the foreboding sound of freedom's price, not the death knell heard in a distant land, but the joyful sounds of freedom surrendered, the sublime sounds of coins pouring out and cashing in freedom's last cent for an infinite treasure.

One may choose whether to believe in God or not. It is a gift freely given. Finding no proof of God, atheists ask one to believe in the miracle that from a complete and absolutely empty vacuum of nothingness, matter sprang forth. Finding no proof of God, believers ask one to believe in the miracle that God chose to create the universe in order to bring forth the possibility of life and love. The great irony in this choice is that the atheist is the very proof that he seeks. The atheist is the proof that the separation is real; the choice is real; freedom is real. Were it otherwise, the proof of God would eliminate the choice. Without that freedom, love cannot exist.

It is affirmed, therefore, that one may choose whether to believe in God, but this proposition is not a mere truism. Rather, it is an unfathomable profundity. For if one may not choose whether to believe in God, then the God of love is a lie. If one may not choose whether to believe in God, then it must either be because we must believe in Him or that He will not reveal Himself to us. If we must believe, then we are nothing more than abused slaves. If He will not reveal Himself, then we are lost and abandoned, useless chattel in a senseless universe.

Choice, therefore, is the indispensable element and the pinnacle of His creation. In it, we find the essential respect and dignity that is the necessary foundation for all love. Without it, the God of love is an utter fiction.

The tolling of the bell is the call to service, but to hear the bells as the child does is faith. We can all hear the bell toll. From time to time, we do answer, but it repeatedly asks the same question. It is not the question put to Mother Teresa by a reporter, but the one that she put to him:

> "A reporter once asked Mother Teresa, 'When a baby dies alone in a Calcutta alley, where is God?' Her response, 'God is there suffering with that baby. The real question is where are you?'"[34]

The bells of child-like faith, however, were made to answer that call. They are the bells of deep and satisfying joy, the joy of coming home. On Christmas Day, 2013, little eight-year-old Delaney Ann Brown died of a rare leukemia. Her family called her "Laney," and they loved her so very much. They shared her plight with family, friends, and the rest of the world through social media. They tried to afford her the pleasures of fulfilling some childhood dreams in the last stages of her life.

Through the work of Make-A-Wish America and the generosity of a popular and well-known singer, Taylor Swift called her on December 20. It was Laney's last birthday, and she was thrilled with the opportunity to have a real conversation with someone so famous. Laney admired the popular singer, and her spirits were lifted by the thoughtful gift of conversation with this one young woman.

The next night was even more remarkable. On December 21st, ten thousand people crowded outside of her doorstep in West Reading, Pennsylvania to sing her Christmas carols. Delaney could no longer get up from her bed to see them, but she could hear them all. Her last days on earth were spent in the loving care of her family and so many of her spiritual brothers and sisters who reached out to her in those days.[35]

The bell tolled in West Reading that Christmas. The tragedy of one inspired the many. They came to honor the innocent angel dying for our freedoms. They sang the song of hope and love to her and her family, easing her pain, sharing time with her as a sister-in-arms. In their solemn service, in their prayers and solidarity, they also and deeply honored the God of Freedom, Life, and Love.

They could have stayed home and done nothing. They could have persisted in the individual freedoms of a self-centric universe. Instead, they reached out to the other and touched the outstretched hand of God. They heard the bell as the child does and came running.

If only I were God, I would love you enough to create you, allow you to become anything you wish to be, call out to others in your hour of need and invite you home, over and over again, into the everlasting glory of my kingdom.

"Mama! I hear the bells!" the child exclaims. *"Mama! I hear them again!"* he says in wide-eyed astonishment. When these are the bells that are heard, these shimmering bells heard with the wonderment of a child, then the joy of freedom lost is upon you as it was upon Gerard Majella. The world will then watch again with wonder the spectacle of one climbing out of his bedroom window and running down the steep mountain path in his sandals, taking nothing, stopping for nothing, carried along by an overwhelming desire to be in the eternal bonds of divine love.

ACKNOWLEDGMENTS

It is impossible to write a book like this without the help, support and advice of many people. This book took many years to create and bring to publication. I thank all who encouraged me along the way.

In particular, I thank Gia Interlandi, Ginger LoGalbo-Irps, Caryl Tracy, Justin Gaffney, and Ray Weigand. They were the first to read the initial rough draft of this book and encouraged me to continue on. They provided many insights and good suggestions, as well as some excellent resource material. I especially thank Caryl Tracy, who has patiently endured the development of this book from beginning to end. She has allowed me to discuss it with her endlessly and has been an important sounding board for tone and content.

Bridget Chambers deserves my deep gratitude for her positivity and guidance. She has been my editor for both content and structure as we brought the book to another level. I am so thankful that she was with me on this long journey. Her patience, clear advice and confidence in the book were critical to its completion. Her contributions and astute observations were indispensable.

I also give special thanks to those who went out of their way to read the manuscript in its various stages. To Mark Gryska, Gerald Nunnery, Fr. David Simpson O. Carm., Linda Tedesso, and Barbara Weigand. Thank you for your time, your thoughts, and your comments. It is difficult for an author to know if he is communicating effectively without an audience to let him know. I am grateful for your time.

Many thanks and a grateful heart to Mike Kudrna. His enthusiastic support of the concepts and subject matter were a source of continued sustenance. Moreover, he has been my guide and mentor for all aspects of social media – so important in today's world. He also spent many hours creating and maintaining the website for this book.

To my social media team who saved me countless hours of frustration and trouble, with enthusiasm and joy while constructing a social media pathway to provide awareness for this book and its themes. For your daily diligence and expertise, thank you Evelyn Garfias, Rebecca Marting, and Kathleen Rusch.

If one can find a publisher who is patient, confident, highly professional, and a passionate believer in you and your work, then you are lucky indeed. If such a publisher finds you, then you are very blessed. I consider myself lucky and blessed. Thank you, Amy Rice!

Finally, to my parents, siblings, and children, who have always given me all the support I need. They have heard about this project for a long time, and in so many little ways have helped me to see it through. With love and gratitude to my parents, Frank & Letitia, who have instilled in me the faith to write such a book as this.

NOTES

Introduction

1   Saint Augustine – see generally On Free Choice of the Will.

2   Saint Aquinas – see generally Summa Theologica.

3   C.S. Lewis - see generally the Problem of Pain.

4   "Good Friday: Pope does televised Q&A on suffering" – an article posted on Yahoo! News on April 22, 2011. Pope Benedict took calls from all over the world. The article describes one call, in part, as follows: "The first question was from Elena, a 7-year-old Japanese girl who told the pope that many children her age were killed in the March 11 disaster and asked why children have to be so sad. 'I also have the same questions. Why is it this way? Why do you have to suffer so much while others live in ease?' Benedict said. 'And we do not have the answers, but we do know that Jesus suffered as you do, an innocent.' Trying for words of comfort, the pope told her that 'even if we are still sad, God is by your side.'"

5   On June 16, 2005 Billy Graham appeared on Larry King's nightly show on CNN for an interview. A short excerpt from the interview follows:
"KING: When you see a tsunami, that doesn't cause you to question God, either?
GRAHAM: No, but I ask why. But I don't know why.
KING: But you don't get an answer.
GRAHAM: No.
KING: But you don't question his…
GRAHAM: I believe that God is in control. In some mysterious way that I don't understand, God allows it. I don't think he sends a tsunami or a hurricane or a Tornado. I think he allows it."

6   PBS Documentary - Frontline: Confessions of Faith and Doubt at Ground Zero, September 3, 2002, produced by Helen Whitney.

7   Mike Conklin, "Reflections of God and Man After a Disaster." Chicago Tribune article January 5, 2005.

8   G.K. Chesterton, *Orthodoxy* (Image Books/Doubleday 2001 edition) p.79.

9   Friedrich Nietzsche – see generally *Thus Spoke Zarathustra, Beyond Good and Evil.*

Chapter 1 – Genesis

1   Genesis Rewritten: The language of this description is based on and reformulated from a narrated visual depiction in the series "The Universe" by the History Channel, 2007.

2   "The Fine Tuning of The Universe" as revised by Dr. Gerald Schroeder, www.2001principle.net with references to the BC Science Documentary, "The Anthropic Principle," 1987.

3   Gottfried Leibniz, *Theodicy*, (1710).

4   Voltaire, *Candide*, (1759). The protagonist, Professor Pangloss, a Job-like figure, is very often heard to say, "all is for the best in the best of all worlds" as he encounters many disasters. One of these disasters is the Lisbon earthquake of 1755 mentioned in Chapter 2 of this book.

5   Isaac Newton, *Principia*, (1687).

6   Albert Einstein – My primary source of information on his life and basic theory is Einstein, by Walter Isaacson, Simon & Schuster Paperbacks, 2008).

7   Brian Greene, *The Elegant Universe*, (First Vintage Books, March, 2000), p. 67.

8   Brian Greene, *The Elegant Universe*, (First Vintage Books, March, 2000), p. 71

9   Brian Greene, *The Elegant Universe*, (First Vintage Books, March, 2000), pp. 75-76

10   Brian Greene, *The Elegant Universe*, (First Vintage Books, March, 2000), p. 82.

11   Brian Greene, *The Elegant Universe*, (First Vintage Books, March, 2000), p. 119.

12   Brian Greene, *The Elegant Universe*, (First Vintage Books, March, 2000), p.114.

13   Brian Greene, *The Elegant Universe*, (First Vintage Books, March, 2000), p.114.

14 Brian Greene, *The Elegant Universe*, (First Vintage Books, March, 2000), p. 136.

15 Brian Greene, *The Elegant Universe*, (First Vintage Books, March, 2000), p. 143.

16 Brian Greene, *The Elegant Universe*, (First Vintage Books, March, 2000), p. 139.

17 "The Fine Tuning of The Universe" as revised by Dr. Gerald Schroeder, www.2001principle.net with references to the BC Science Documentary, "The Anthropic Principle," 1987.

18 Stephen Hawking, *A Brief History of Time*, (Bantam Books 1990), p. 125. Note that I have inserted the phrase "(for the constants)" into Hawking's original quotation for the purpose of contextual clarity. Hawking refers to them as "fundamental numbers" in his preceding sentence.

19 "The Fine Tuning of The Universe" as revised by Dr. Gerald Schroeder, www.2001principle.net with references to the BC Science Documentary, "The Anthropic Principle," 1987.

20 "The Fine Tuning of The Universe" as revised by Dr. Gerald Schroeder, www.2001principle.net with references to the BC Science Documentary, "The Anthropic Principle," 1987.

21 Carl Sagan, Introduction to *A Brief History of Time*, by Stephen Hawking (Bantam Books 1990).

22 Stephen Hawking, *A Brief History of Time*, (Bantam Books 1990), p. 175.

23 Brian Greene, *The Elegant Universe*, (First Vintage Books, March 2000), p. 366.

24 Brian Greene, *The Elegant Universe*, (First Vintage Books, March 2000), p. 385.

25 Paul Davies, *The Mind of God*, (Simon & Schuster Paperbacks 2005). 15.

26 26. C.S. Lewis, *The Problem of Pain*, (HarperCollins Publishers 2001 Edition), pp. 116-117.

27 C.S. Lewis, *The Problem of Pain*, (HarperCollins Publishers 2001 Edition), pp. 25-26.

28 C.S. Lewis, "The Efficacy of Prayer."

29 Genesis, Chapter 1, Verse 31; the exact quote is: "God looked at everything he had made, and he found it very good."

30 Genesis, Chapter 1, Verse 27; the exact quote is: "God created man in his image; in the divine image he created him; male and female he created them."

Chapter 2 – My God, My God, Why Have You Forsaken Me?

1 Mark Twain, No.44, The Mysterious Stranger, (University of California Press 1969) pp. 186-187.

2 2. Mark Twain, The Mysterious Stranger, (Harper & Brothers 1922) p. 26.

3 Taken from an astute essay about Mark Twain's Mysterious Stranger. The essay was written by Bruce Michelson and entitled "Deus Ludens: The Shaping of Mark Twain's Mysterious Stranger," originally found in "Novel: A Forum on Fiction, Autumn 1980, Vol. 14, No. 1" (Duke University Press Autumn 1980), p. 48.

4 Most of the facts cited and some of the language regarding the historic tragedies are taken from: Lesley Newson, *Devastation! The World's Worst Natural Disasters*, (DK Publishing 1998).

5 Mark Twain, No.44, *The Mysterious Stranger*, (University of California Press 1969) pp. 187.

Chapter 3 – Paradise Lost

1 G.K. Chesterton, *Orthodoxy* (Image Books/Doubleday 2001 edition) p.63.

2 G.K. Chesterton, *Orthodoxy* (Image Books/Doubleday 2001 edition) p.80.

3 Francis Collins, *The Language of God* (Free Press – a Division of Simon & Schuster 2006) p. 195

4 G.K. Chesterton, *Orthodoxy* (Image Books/Doubleday 2001 edition) p.78.

5 5. This "quote" attributed to C.S. Lewis is a fusion of the prior quotes from endnote 27 in Chapter 1: "Try to exclude the possibility of suffering which the order of nature and the existence of free wills involve, and you find that you have excluded life

itself." / "Perhaps this isn't the 'best of all possible' universes, but the only possible one."

6   Stephen Hawking, *A Brief History of Time*, (Bantam Books 1990), p. 125.

Chapter 4 – Our Father Who Art in Heaven

1   C.S. Lewis, *The Problem of Pain*, (HarperCollins Publishers 2001 Edition), p. 130.

2   Alison Gopnik, *The Philosophical Baby*, (Farrar, Straus and Giroux 2009), p. 6.

3   Alison Gopnik, *The Philosophical Baby*, (Farrar, Straus and Giroux 2009), p. 17.

4   C.S. Lewis – "We meet no ordinary people in our lives." This is a commonly used paraphrase from a quote taken from his book *The Weight of Glory*, (Harper One, 2001) pp. 45-46. The actual quote is, "There are no ordinary people. You have never talked to a mere mortal."

5   Alison Gopnik, *The Philosophical Baby*, (Farrar, Straus and Giroux 2009), p. 123.

6   Alison Gopnik, *The Philosophical Baby*, (Farrar, Straus and Giroux 2009), p. 119.

7   Alison Gopnik, *The Philosophical Baby*, (Farrar, Straus and Giroux 2009), p. 91.

8   Alison Gopnik, *The Philosophical Baby*, (Farrar, Straus and Giroux 2009), p. 71.

9   Alison Gopnik, *The Philosophical Baby*, (Farrar, Straus and Giroux 2009), p. 105.

10   Alison Gopnik, *The Philosophical Baby*, (Farrar, Straus and Giroux 2009), p. 195.

11   Francis S. Collins, *The Language of God*, (Free Press – a division of Simon & Schuster, 2006), p. 215.

12   Francis S. Collins, *The Language of God*, (Free Press – a division of Simon & Schuster, 2006), pp. 216-217.

13   Francis S. Collins, *The Language of God*, (Free Press – a division of Simon & Schuster, 2006), p. 217.

Chapter 5 – The Greatest of These Is Love

1   Friedrich Nietzsche – "an overflowing of the soul" – cited by Will Durant in a footnote in *The Story of Philosophy*, Parker Books, a Division of Simon & Schuster 1953) p. 421. See also Friedrich Nietzsche, Beyond Good and Evil,(Millennium Publications 2014), p. 41 –"in true love it is the soul that envelops the body."

2   Lee Hill Kavanaugh, "35 minutes to live, feel love," (McClatchy/Tribune Newspapers), appearing in the Chicago Tribune on May 3, 2007.

Chapter 6 – The Big Bang

1   Nicolas Cheetham, *Universe*, (Quercus, 2005), was a source of some of the information on our solar system.

2   An interesting article about the buffalo is posted online at medium.com/@davidbunnell. In it, he quotes from a letter written in 1871 by an American soldier named George Anderson, who was travelling through Kansas. The portion of the letter quoted states as follows: "I am safe in calling this a single herd, but it is impossible to approximate the millions that composed it. It took me six days on horseback to ride through it."

3   Rachael Bale, "How Many Species Haven't We Found Yet?" National Geographic, December 26, 2019.

4   G.K. Chesterton, Orthodoxy (Image Books/Doubleday 2001 edition). The whole idea of Chesterton's approach to the joy and celebration of existence is nicely described in Philip Yancy's splendid introduction to the 2001 edition of Orthodoxy. The introduction is entitled "G. K. Chesterton: Prophet of Mirth" and includes the following Chesterton poem:

"Here dies another day
During which I have had eyes, ears hands
And the great world round me;
And with tomorrow begins another.
Why am I allowed two?"

5   Annie Dillard, *Pilgrim at Tinker Creek*, (Harper Collins Perennial Modern Classics Edition, 2007), p. 11.

6   G.K. Chesterton, Orthodoxy (Image Books/Doubleday 2001 edition) p.58.

Chapter 7 – Where Two or Three Are Gathered in His Name

1   Annie Dillard, *Holy the Firm*, (HarperCollins Perennial Library 2003 edition) p.55. I love this phrase from her short and glorious book, Holy the Firm – a book I highly recommend as a deeply insightful, emotional and spiritual exploration of the problem of pain and suffering.

2   Soren Kierkegaard, *Purity of Heart is to Will One Thing*, (Harper One 2008) p 184.

3   Father Edward Saint-Omer C.SS.R., *St. Gerard Majella*, (Tan Books & Publishers, Inc. 2012 Edition), pp. 152-153.

4   St. Therese of Lisieux, *The Story of a Soul*, (Aziloth Books 2018) p. 90. See also: *The Essential Wisdom of the Saints*, edited by Carol Kelly-Gangi, (Fall River Pres 2008), p.30.

5   James Martin, S.J., *My Life with The Saints*, (Loyola Press 2006), p. 151.

6   G.K. Chesterton, *What's Wrong with The World*, (Dover Publications, Inc. 2007) p. 29.

7   St. Therese of Lisieux, The Story of a Soul, (Aziloth Books 2018) pp. 11-12. See also: James Martin, S.J., My Life with The Saints, (Loyola Press 2006), p. 36.

8   Soren Kierkegaard, Journals.

9   "Thus it is said that there is only one thing greater than freedom and that is dependence on God – who died twice for freedom – in Creation and on the Cross." I reference this here to avoid any confusion on what is meant by dying for freedom in Creation. I simply mean to state that His act of creation was a sort of death to His free and active involvement with beings of free will – i.e., the necessary principles of separation we have been discussing throughout the book.

10   Annie Dillard, Holy the Firm, (HarperCollins Perennial Library 2003 edition)p. 62.

11   Soren Kierkegaard, *Fear and Trembling / The Sickness unto Death*, (DoubleDay and Company 1954), p.131 – Epilogue to Fear and Trembling.

12   Mirabai Starr, Introduction to *The Interior Castle*, by St. Teresa of Avila, as translated by Mirabai Starr, (Riverhead Books, The Berkley Publishing Group 2003), pp 1-3.

13   Plato, *Apology*, 38a.

14   Soren Kierkegaard, *Purity of Heart is to Will One Thing*, (Harper One 2008) p 197-198.

15   Saint Padre Pio, *Essential Wisdom of the Saints*, edited and compiled by Carol Kelly-Gangi, (Fall River Press 2008), p. 63.

16   C.S. Lewis, The Problem of Pain, (HarperCollins Edition 2001), p. 62.

17   Soren Kierkegaard, *Fear and Trembling / The Sickness unto Death*, (DoubleDay and Company 1954), p.142 – Preface to *The Sickness unto Death*.

18   Mirabai Starr, Introduction to *The Interior Castle*, by St. Teresa of Avila, as translated by Mirabai Starr, (Riverhead Books, The Berkley Publishing Group 2003), p 14.

19   Soren Kierkegaard, The Journals of Kierkegaard, 1834 – 1854.

Chapter 8 – For Whom the Bell Tolls

1   The statement by the WWII veteran was taken from the PBS Documentary, "Hallowed Grounds," directed by Robert Uth, 2009.

2   With apologies to John Donne and his poem "For Whom the Bell Tolls" originally found in his Meditation 17 from his work entitled *Devotions Upon Emergent Occassions*.

"No man is an island,
Entire of itself.
Each is a piece of the continent,
A part of the main.
If a clod be washed away by the sea,
Europe is the less.
As well as if a promontory were.

As well as if a manor of thine own
Or of thine friend's were.
Each man's death diminishes me,
For I am involved in mankind.
Therefore, send not to know
For whom the bell tolls,
It tolls for thee."

Chapter 9 - Suffering Servants

1   All of the information regarding the tragic story of Natasha McShane comes from a series of articles in the Chicago Tribune as reported by the following reporters on the following dates:

04/24/2010 Duaa Eldeib & William Lee; "Man with bat attacks women in Bucktown: Pair seriously injured, victim able to describe assailant"

04/28/2010 William Lee, Todd Lightly; "2 charged in bat attack" & Annie Sweeney

05/03/2010 Kristen Mack; "Victim of Bat attack open eyes, still in a coma"

05/10/2010 No byline given; "Bars raising funds for 2 hurt in bat attack"

05/17/2010 No byline given; "Bat-beating victim is moved to rehab center"

05/20/2010 No byline given; "Suspects face more charges in bat attack"

06/04/2010 No byline given; "Bat beating victim starting to speak"

06/11/2010 Carlos Sadovi; "Bucktown beating victim improving"

06/14/2010 Cynthia Dizikes; "Bat beating victim making progress: Family says rehabbing woman has been able to recognize her mom"

07/13/2010 No byline given; "Beating victim returns to Ireland"

04/21/2011 No byline given; "Bucktown Bat Beating: One Year Later: Exchange student back in Northern Ireland, can't walk or talk following vicious attack"

04/18/2010 Colleen Mastony; "2 years later, beating victim still struggling: Student in Bucktown attack regresses in Northern Ireland, but family hangs on"

04/23/2013 Colleen Mastony; "Family awaits justice in attack"

07/10/2013 Colleen Mastony & Steve Schmadeke; "Driver pleads guilty in baseball-bat attack"

10/14/2013 Colleen Mastony & Steve Schmadeke "Bucktown bat-beating trial to begin"

10/17/2013 Steve Schmadeke; "Bat-beating victim speaks"

10/25/2013 Steve Schmadeke; "Guilty verdict in ball bat beating"

05/18/2014 Colleen Mastony; "A voice for Natasha"

05/23/2014 Steve Schmadeke; "90 years for Bucktown baseball bat beatings"

2   Christopher DeVinck, *The Power of the Powerless*, (Crossword Publishing Company 1988), pp. 85-88.

3   Christopher DeVinck, *The Power of the Powerless*, (Crossword Publishing Company 1988), p. 88.

4   Christopher DeVinck, *The Power of the Powerless*, (Crossword Publishing Company 1988), pp. 105-106.

Chapter 10 – Into Your Hands We Commend Our Spirits

1   James Martin, S.J., *My Life with The Saints*, (Loyola Press 2006), p. 164.

2   Mirabai Starr, Introduction to *The Interior Castle*, by St. Teresa of Avila, as translated by Mirabai Starr, (Riverhead Books, The Berkley Publishing Group 2003), p 10.

3   Father Edward Saint-Omer C.SS.R., *St. Gerard Majella*, (Tan Books & Publishers, Inc. 2012 Edition), pp. 2-3.

4   Father Edward Saint-Omer C.SS.R., *St. Gerard Majella*, (Tan Books & Publishers, Inc. 2012 Edition), p. 4.

5   Father Edward Saint-Omer C.SS.R., *St. Gerard Majella*, (Tan Books & Publishers, Inc. 2012 Edition), p. 12.

6   Ibid., p. 13.

7   Ibid., p. 14.

8   Ibid., p. 20.

9   Ibid., p. 21.

10   Ibid., p. 28.

11   Ibid., p. 17.

12   Ibid., p. 61

13   Ibid., pp. 122-123.

14   Ibid., p. 163.

15   Ibid., p. 156.

16   Ibid., p. 158.

17   Ibid., p. 151.

18   Ibid., p. 71.

19   Ibid., p. 72.

20   Ibid., p. 73.

21   Ibid., p. 160.

22   Ibid., p. 83.

23   Ibid., p. 83.

24   Ibid., pp. 153-154.

25   Ibid., p. 90.

26   The source of this quote was from a detailed article found at SaintGerard.com. The site no longer carries this article and many no longer be the same site where the article was posted.

27   Many of the above stories regarding St. Gerard Majella and stories about his life and legacy can also be found in the video, "St. Gerard Majella," (Human Life International, 2001).

28   Father Edward Saint-Omer C.SS.R., St. Gerard Majella, (Tan Books & Publishers, Inc. 2012 Edition), p. 179.

29   Father Edward Saint-Omer C.SS.R., St. Gerard Majella, (Tan Books & Publishers, Inc. 2012 Edition), p. 39

30   Ibid., p. 39.

31   Ibid., p. 40.

32   Ibid., p. 40.

33   Ibid., p. 42.

34   John G. Stackhouse Jr., "Can God Be Trusted?" (Oxford University Press 2000), P. 67.

35   In the last days of Delaney Brown's young life, many came to support her. The following YouTube videos beautifully depict the amazing respect many of her friends and neighbors had for her and for her family as they tried to provide Laney the comfort she sought at the end of her life:

Carols for Laney Brown

Laney Brown's Wish

Pennsylvania Girl Delaney Brown Who Inspired Thousands to Come

6,000 People go Caroling for a Girl with Cancer

Dying Girl's Christmas Wish

ABOUT THE COVER ARTIST

Pablo Carlos Budassi is an artist, musician, designer, and creator who has traveled the world contributing to myriad projects that speak to his soul. For more than three decades, his music and illustrations have been featured throughout several countries, including Argentina, Guatemala, Turkey, Sweden and the United States. His special interests in human rights, physics, and philosophy have bred a career stemmed in conveying the complexity of the world through art, music, and poetry. He currently resides in Mendoza, Argentina.